Doing the impossible together with God

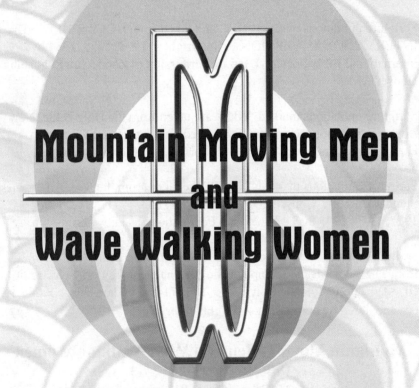

Mountain Moving Men and Wave Walking Women

Rudi & Sharon Swanepoel

Mountain Moving Men and Wave Walking Women

ISBN 978-0-9772647-7-3

P. O. Box 1430, Dacula, GA 30019

www.GodsGlory.org

Table of Contents

Endorsements

This newest book that Rudi and Sharon have written will challenge the reader to take a closer look at what a Biblical marriage is supposed to be about. The insights are practical and humorous, but always faith building and motivating. It's hard to find a book that both men and women can enjoy. This is one of those books you won't want to put down, regardless of your gender. Be blessed!

Dr. Randy Valimont

Senior Pastor, Griffin First Assembly, Griffin, Georgia

In "Mountain Moving Men and Wave Walking Women" authors Rudi & Sharon Swanepoel take on the formidable task of helping us build a strong, healthy, enduring marriage in a culture that is hell bent on the destruction of marriage and marriages. Rudi is indeed a mountain moving man and Sharon a wave walking woman. Their marriage is a wonderful living, breathing example of the truths and principles laid out in this book. My childhood sweetheart Kathie has been my lovely bride for nearly four decades. I only wish I had the lessons laid out in the Swanepoel's book before making so many mistakes as a young, naïve husband. Read, enjoy, and put into practice "Mountain Moving Men and Wave Walking Women" and let's show the world marriage works when you follow the Master's plan.

Pastors David and Kathie Thomas
Lead Pastors Victory Christian Center, Youngstown, Ohio
President, Next Level Leadership Network

The content of this book is more than just theory. It comes both from experience and from God's written plan for marriage as found in the scriptures. Rudi and Sharon Swanepoel provide a truly fresh perspective concerning the uniqueness of men and women and how to maximize each other's assets as two become one. It is obvious that "Mountain Moving Men and Wave Walking Women" is an extension of their ministry and readers will enjoy their candidness and down-to-earth presentation. Their insights in this book will be helpful to every reader.

Pastor Michael and Cathy Petrucci
Senior Pastor, Praise Assembly, Newark, Delaware

You are about to gain some amazing revelation into God's divine plan for marriage. Mountain Moving Men and Wave Walking Women is a book that I believe will provide biblical understanding and new hope for a lot of marriages. Get ready to go to a new level in intimacy, romance, and spiritual power as you become mountain moving men and wave walking women.

Pastors Chuck and Barbara Farina
Lead Pastors of New Hope Church, Abilene, Texas

Rudi and Sharon have been our dearest friends and associates for many years. During this time we have admired how beautifully they ministered together but more importantly, we have seen the same love and affection they have for one another publicly, demonstrated in their daily life. They are truly the "real deal" when it comes to a witness of what a Christ-centered marriage is and hence, very well qualified to share with others the joys of Christian marriage. Couples reading this book together will be blessed as they apply the tips and truths contained herein to their marriage.

Pastor Bill and Lynna Roberts
Senior Pastor, Christ Chapel, Woodbridge, Virginia.

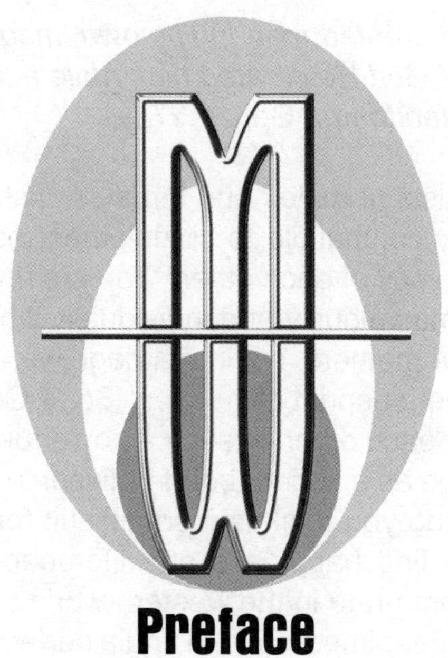

Preface

The blueprint of heaven for men and women is to be Mountain Moving Men and Wave Walking Women. Never to be overwhelmed by what seems to be too immovable or turbulent.

God created men and women for Himself and for each other. Our origin is divine! We are much more than mere physical beings, we are primarily spiritual beings and our destiny is to live to the fullest potential God has placed in us. God is calling every man to be a mountain mover and every woman to be a wave walker, living beyond the realm of the natural. In fact, we carry God's fingerprints on our lives. We are a result of His handiwork. But do not just take our word for it, take Him at His word:

> *"So God created man in His own image; in the image of God He created him; male and female He created them."* Gen. 1:27

Humanity consists of males and females, distinct in so many ways yet totally compatible to complement each other. As a couple we often say of each other, "You are my better half." In birth we were marvelously and individually woven together in the womb of our mothers, but in marriage we were completed according to the blueprint of heaven. So, if God made us for Himself and for each other, in such a powerful way that He instituted marriage as a sacred bond between a man and woman.[1] Why then do you think is it so difficult for so many men and women to find happiness and life-peace in marriage? Why is the divorce-rate in the western world so unacceptably high? Why is it near impossible to find a perfect "better-half" to share life with and why is it so frustratingly challenging to be someone's "better-half" today? There are so many questions surrounding marriage that need to be answered. Our prayer is that you will find scriptural answers to these and other questions as we journey through this book together.

Our marriage has been a tremendously blissful adventure that started on December 16, 1989, for which we are eternally grateful to the Lord Jesus Christ. He has led us on life's journey from young "whippersnapper" students to a wonderfully blessed and established family unit with the smile of heaven over our lives. We have navigated through many challenges life has brought and we learned how to identify and avoid those slick temptations designed to cause us to veer off the right road and end in a destructive ditch. We have managed

---

1 *Genesis 2:22-24, "Then the rib which the LORD God had taken from man He made into a woman, and He brought her to the man. And Adam said: "This [is] now bone of my bones And flesh of my flesh; She shall be called Woman, Because she was taken out of Man." Therefore a man shall leave his father and mother and be joined to his wife, and they shall become one flesh." NKJV*

to extend our honeymoon and frankly, there is no end in sight. Hardly a week goes by that someone, strangers included, will not comment on how "in love" we still are. Truth being it is hard to keep it a secret that we really like each other and are committed to God's fullest for our lives.

Our story is not exclusively unique. You too can find true happiness in who you are and with whom you are. You too can experience what we have, what God intended for you from the very beginning. God made us man and woman, and in this book we will explore what that truly means. We will look at powerful principles that will propel you into a new frontier of successful living. Whether you are a man or a woman, a happily married couple or a relationally challenged struggler, this book is for you.

Mountain Moving Men and Wave Walking Women is not an innovative idea but rather an important inspiration to men and woman of all ages. While driving in Virginia, on our way to a speaking engagement, the Lord stirred in our hearts and started to unlock the principles we are about to share with you in this book. We have been asked many times to identify and document some of the things we have discovered over the years of serving God together, but what the Lord gave us in the car that day was much more than mere personal opinions and humanistic logic. It was inspired revelation. The title says it all! God has given every man and woman a supernatural element that makes them capable of accomplishing the impossible. Jesus said if you have faith like a mustard seed you can move mountains.[2] He also encouraged a disciple to walk on water, not to look at the waves but keep his faith activated and his focus on Jesus.[3]

This book will challenge you to be who God made you to be. Not to merely conform to what is acceptable in pop culture or

---

2 Matthew 17:20
3 Matthew 14:28-31

society as a whole but to be transformed into the exquisite being He made you to be. We have approached this book from a Biblical view so even if some may find us not to be politically correct[4], they will discover that we endeavored to be scripturally sound.

You will learn to move mountains and walk on waves as you explore God's ultimate plan for your life in the pages of this book. You will discover the marvelous supernatural qualities He has placed in you and experience its impact in your marriage, relationships, career, finances and family.

No, we have not yet gained perfection in marriage or reached the highest pinnacle of relational bliss. We have however discovered a way to keep climbing together, enjoying each other while achieving the impossible together with God. Each day is an adventure in learning more about God, each other and the fullness of His destiny for us.

Our prayer is that your faith-level be lifted. Let your now activated faith result in you and your spouse doing the impossible together with God.

---

4 Political correctness tries to accommodate and appease everybody regardless of faith or moral fiber.

Chapter 1: Origin

Molded Men And Woven Women

Let's start at the beginning, the origin of man. According to the Bible, man was created by God. In fact, we are the crown of God's creation. We read in Psalm 8:4-6,

> *"When I consider Your heavens, the work of Your fingers, The moon and the stars, which You have ordained,* ***What is man that You are mindful of him, And the son of man that You visit him?*** *For You have made him a little*

lower than the angels, And You have crowned him with glory and honor. You have made him to have dominion over the works of Your hands; You have put all things under his feet," (Emphasis added)

God created everything with you in mind -- the splendor of nature, the rotation of the planets, and even the moon and the stars in the sky! He prepared this world for his *magnum opus*[1]. If we look at creation we find that men and women are in a class of their own.[2] Before Adam and Eve were created God spoke everything into existence with His voice. Although the Lord also voiced His intentions to create man, he took the creative process further.

Molded Men

God had to roll up His sleeves and get His hands dirty with Adam. He formed or molded man. It is as if His words would not be enough this time.[3] The Hebrew word used for *"formed"* here is *"yatzar"*[4] and it means *"to mold into a form; especially as a potter; to press through the squeezing into shape"*. As a man Adam was molded into a form, taking on a clay replica of the image of God.[5] He started as clay in the hands of the Master Potter. This reminds us of the eighteenth chapter in the book of Jeremiah. The prophet went down to the potter's house. God instructed him to go there so He could speak to Jeremiah. The potter was making an object of clay on the

Your life was designed and formed by the Lord

---

1 From Latin magnum, "large" and opus, "work"; a person's greatest work / masterpiece (dictionary.com)

2 Psalm 8:5 "*For You have made him a little lower than the angels, and You have crowned him with glory and honor.*"

3 Genesis 2:7 NKJV "*And the Lord God formed man of the dust of the ground, and breathed into his nostrils the breath of life; and the man became a living soul.*"

4 Strong's Dictionary of Hebrew Word: H#03335

5 Genesis 1:27

wheel, but at first what he was making seemed like a failed attempt because the clay was corrupted. Thankfully the potter did not give up, but formed another object, something that carried his approval.

Men today must realize that a pile of dirt on the ground is nothing special, but that same dirt in the hands of the Master Potter can be molded into something special. Clay is a dirty medium to work with. It will dirty your hands and is not very costly. Maybe that is where the phrase "dirt cheap" came from. Dirt is cheap. A man's original raw material may be nothing special. Men, you may even feel like all you have to offer in this life is dirt with some trace elements of iron and minerals. God's alchemy and chemistry yielded a perfect blend of natural materials, minerals and atoms. We have great news for you! Your worth is not measured by the splendor of the raw substance in you, but by the Name of the Artist that forms you! Once you realize that you are a divine original you will look at yourself differently. A Picasso can sell for several million dollars, simply because it is an authentic Picasso. Without that name it is simply an ordinary cloth with some paint on it. Without the touch of God in your life you are nothing more than a clump of clay.

Do not allow the fingerprints of the enemy on your life. You may not be able to choose your raw, original material, i.e., your gifts, abilities, DNA, strengths and weaknesses, but you can choose who you will trust to fashion these qualities in your life. Place yourself in the hands of the Master. Let Him mold you. Allow Him to squeeze you into the form He designed for you. You were not a mere surprise or a bundle of joy for your parents. Your life was designed and formed by the Lord. Just like with the clay in Jeremiah 18, at times you might feel like God's first attempt with you failed. Maybe the pressures of life have bent you out of shape. Or you sometimes feel like soggy clay that cannot be true to form, struggling to live up to the expectations others have of you. There are things that can corrupt the structure of your clay. The Bible calls them the works of the flesh.

> *"When you follow the desires of your sinful nature, the results are very clear: sexual immorality, impurity, lustful pleasures, idolatry, sorcery, hostility, quarreling, jealousy, outbursts of anger, selfish ambition, dissension, division, envy, drunkenness, wild parties, and other sins like these. Let me tell you again, as I have before, that anyone living that sort of life will not inherit the Kingdom of God."* [6]

These things interfere with the true purpose of your life and will be the very things that push you further away from the Creator. The beauty of being clay is that the Master Potter can reshape, reform, and remold you. His fingerprints will be embedded in your character and the grooves of His hands wrapping around your life, fashioning your form. Then He will glaze you with His glory, firing your destiny in the kiln, your soul with the power of His Spirit. He truly is the God of second chances, our God who loves and welcomes the challenge to make improvements in your life.

The Bible calls this makeover of the original clay *"to be born again"*. With your old, sinful life filling your heart with regret, disappointments, and evil emotions, God gives you a way to start over.

> *"Therefore, if anyone is in Christ, he is a new creation; old things have passed away; behold, all things have become new."* [7]

If you want to step into the supernatural and become a mountain mover you must be a molded man, made and molded ac-

---

6 Galatians 5:18-21 NLT
7 2 Corinthians 5:17 NKJV

cording to God's design for your life and not merely living according to your own plans. A Molded Man has been prepared for supernatural living and success from the very beginning! Remember, when God finished molding Adam He breathed into him the breath of life and that's when Adam became a living being. God will form you and mold you into His image. But you cannot be all form and no breath, you need spirit to power your form, spirit that comes from the Creator Himself. How can a clump of clay ever be truly successful? Only when it is surrenders into the hands of the Master Potter and allows his life to be powered by a spirit supernaturally installed and activated by the Lord.

Make something special and remarkable of your life. Be a molded dad, husband, employee or entrepreneur. Being cast in the form God envisioned you in will cause opportunity and success to knock on your door. You'll be able to move previously immovable mountains and obstacles in your life. You may have started as a clump of clay but today you are a living being. Make the most of what the Lord has placed in you. A keyword in the life of a Molded Man is "surrender". Stubborn clay is not pliable. Hard clay clings to the old previously fashioned form, unable to be formed anew. A Molded Man takes on the character and nature of the One who made him.

Make something remarkable of your life!

Woven Women

Men and women are quite different on almost every level. Sure we are all human beings, but that is about where our similarities end. Have you ever wondered why? Is it simply because of individual personality traits or physiological processes in our bodies? Is it a mere hormonal or chromosome thing? When we look at how God created women we find answers to these questions. After Adam was molded from the dust of the earth he was alone. God said,

> *"It is not good for man to be alone; I will make him a helper comparable to him."* [8]

God needed to make another human being, someone that would be a *"helper comparable"* to Adam. You would think that the Lord would need more clay, another mold and some breath. That is the material He used with Adam. But God had other plans.

> *"He caused a deep sleep to fall upon Adam, and as he slept God took one of his ribs, and from the rib He made a woman and brought her unto the man."* [9]

To make a perfect woman, someone that would be 100% compatible with and suitable for Adam, God would have to come up with someone extraordinary. He took something that was a sure fit, one of Adam's own ribs, as a starting point. No matter what the end product would look like, at her core she would be a perfect match for Adam. There would be no reason for rejection. She would not be a misfit or an outsider. God's creation of Eve was truly a masterpiece.

It is in the time spent with God that His ideas and plans for you are established

Look at Adam's response:

> *"This is now bone of my bones, and flesh of my flesh: she shall be called Woman, because she was taken out of Man."* [10]

Someone jokingly said he knew why women are called *"women"*. When Adam woke up from the deep sleep and saw the beautiful creature God just made he was smitten and gasped,

8 Genesis 2:18 NKJV
9 Genesis 2:21 NKJV
10 Genesis 2:23

"Wow! Man!"

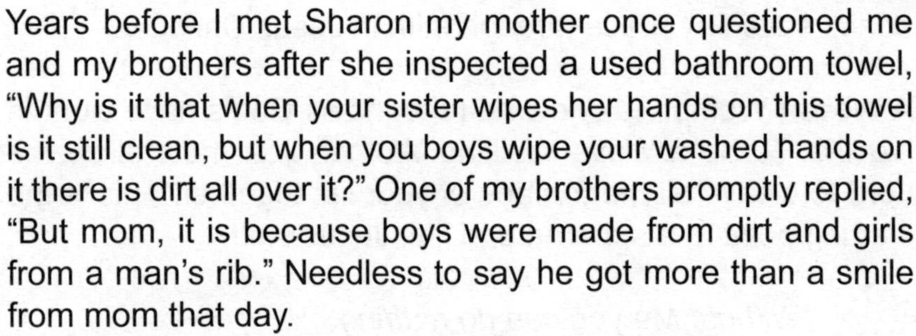

Years before I met Sharon my mother once questioned me and my brothers after she inspected a used bathroom towel, "Why is it that when your sister wipes her hands on this towel is it still clean, but when you boys wipe your washed hands on it there is dirt all over it?" One of my brothers promptly replied, "But mom, it is because boys were made from dirt and girls from a man's rib." Needless to say he got more than a smile from mom that day.

Although the Lord *"formed"* the man, He *"made"* the woman. The Hebrew word for *"made"* literally means *"to build" or "to begin to build"*[11]. It implies that God spent more time on the creation of the woman. First He took material that He already worked on in the creation of Adam as a starting point. Then he *"began to build"* Eve. Few people would dispute the general differences between men and women. Women tend to be more intuitive than men. They have a greater understanding and see things in a different light than men do. Can it be that because the Lord spent more time creating the woman that she has more detailed "wiring" and presents a more complex being than the man? We think so. Think of a woman as being woven by the hand of God. The Master embroider fashioned a delicate, masterful and detailed being by threading the fibers of her body, soul and spirit together. He did all this with the man in mind; after all He was creating a helper comparable to Adam. He wove, wrought and created until every detail was perfect and then presented this woven woman to the molded man.

A Woven Woman is not someone formed or woven merely at birth, she is someone woven into Christ. The tapestry of her life will not be complete without the red thread of the precious blood of Jesus that washes away her sin and life's stain. Her

---

11 Strong's Concordance of Hebrew Words H#01129 - banah - means "to build".

life is threaded together with Christ's ability and love. Both Molded Men and Woven Women are made new by being born again, saved by grace through faith in Jesus Christ.

A Woven Woman is one who recognizes God's handiwork in her life. To be a Wave Walking Woman you must allow the Lord to weave all the threads of your life together. This is the starting point to a supernatural life. Jesus said,

> *"Without Me you can do nothing."* [12]

As a Woven Women you realize that without the personal touch and continued maintenance and influence of your Creator, your life would become impossibly complicated and your true function and purpose hopelessly distorted. You'll never reach the realm of the supernatural without the amazing touch of the Master's hand. A Woven Woman is a woman who finds true freedom in the comforting relationship she has with Almighty God. As a Woven Woman you realize that you are a divine work in progress, an increasingly elaborate masterpiece woven to reflect the Creator's splendor and grandeur, God's tapestry that brings definition, purpose and promise to lost humanity.

Woven Women are intricate beings. They process life in a unique way. Overall they are more detailed and deeper than men. Their views are deeper and their emotional fabric more complex.

How do I become a Woven Woman? Exposure to the Master Weaver Himself will present you with a life designed and altered for success. It is in the time spent with God that His ideas and plans for you are established, instead of the ideas of man and the altering actions of others in your life. Many times problems can be woven into your life, like the opinion of others. Think of it as a fashion designer. Your identity should not

---

12 John 15:4-6

be founded or shaped by the interference of people in your life or by replicating family traits. Family traits are secondary in your life. Your authenticity comes from the One who designed your patterns, picked the threads and wove your life together. Renew your mind by discovering God's thoughts over you. Catch a glimpse of His design for your life. Marvel at His masterpiece by celebrating His stitching and woven genius in your life. You are not what others say you are. Show them the divine pattern and fabric of your life. Allow Him to weave His strong threads of integrity and purpose into your character. Give people a glimpse of God in the way you react to circumstances and interact with others. You can wear a Calvin Klein design, but you remain a God original, one of a kind! You may have family traits resembling your mother or father, but you are a unique original crafted according to Heaven's pattern to fit the shape of God's destiny for your life. If the fabric of your life is torn or wrinkled in the tough circumstances of life, then allow the Master Weaver to refresh, renew and restore you to your original splendor.

A Molded Man is not better than a Woven Woman merely because man was God's original idea. A Woven Woman is not of greater value to God because He took more time creating her. In fact, there should be no such competition. Both have the fingerprints of God all over their lives. God's purposes for men and women are phenomenally wondrous. The Lord has an order of doing things. He is never outdated or old fashioned. His ways are not restrictive but amazingly liberating and empowering. Understanding His ways, thoughts and purposes will reveal our true purpose and divine destiny.

Understanding His ways, thoughts and purposes will reveal our true purpose and divine destiny

Men, look at your woman as a divine tapestry wrought by the Master Weaver. Celebrate His pattern displayed in her life. Explore the various ways God used to weave her together. You'll find patterns that are uniquely her, God's personal blessing to you. She is your better half. You'll find God's priceless autograph on her life that sets her apart from other women. She's a one of a kind original especially made to match you!

Women, look at your man as marvelously molded by the Master Potter. Celebrate God's form in him. You'll be drawn to the raw masculine material God used to form and fashion his life. If you look with the eye of a potter you'll appreciate the detailed and deliberate work God did to mold him with you in mind. He is your better half too; his strength and quirkiness are strategically placed to warm your heart.

Prayer Application

Dear Heavenly Father
Please help me to remember that I belong to You and that I am fashioned by Your Divine Design. Let me see myself through Your eyes, identifying and reconciling with your blueprint for my life. I yield my life into Your hands to have Your will and Your way in me.
In Jesus Name.
Amen.

Notes:

____

____

____

____

____

____

Chapter 2: Function

Mechanics of Men And Wiring or Women

A man is a Coverer and a woman a Carrier. The Lord stirred this statement in Sharon's spirit one day as we were on our way to a church service. In fact many of the revelations in this book were stirred in the car on our way to that meeting. He continued to reveal this powerful concept of divine order when it comes to men and women.

Look at the letter "M" in man. Do you see the umbrella-like covering shape? It can be an ideal covering to crawl underneath if the "M" is large enough. Now flip the "M" around and you get a "W" as in woman. The umbrella just became a basket like carrier, ideal to carry valuables. It is important how you view your spouse. He or she plays a large role in your life. You simply cannot diminish their place and prominence in your marriage. Make your man big in your life. The bigger he is to you the better he can cover you. Expand your wife's importance in your life and in doing so you will increase her capacity to carry and care for your heart.

Coverer

Just like an umbrella a man is a coverer. He can open up and bring protection from the rain or create a protective shade from the rays of the sun. That same umbrella must be lifted up above what it is supposed to be protecting. To be protected you must come under the umbrella's covering. Lift up your man so he can protect you. Women, do not carry your umbrella as a walking stick in your hand. Lift him up so that he can open up and he can fulfill his role in your life. Husbands, when you are lifted up, it is time to open up and be all that the Lord called you to be. Remember, you are carried by God and your wife.

A coverer establishes an atmosphere where growth can happen.

A coverer establishes an atmosphere where growth can happen. Think of a greenhouse that nurseries use to grow their plants in. A greenhouse is usually made of transparent material that allows the sun in but keeps inclement weather out. It optimizes the atmosphere in which the plants grow and often causes the plants to grow faster and fruit to ripen quicker. Plants are also healthier and stronger coming from a greenhouse. A greenhouse is in effect a covering to the plants. Did you know that one of the main works of the Holy Spirit is that of a covering? In Genesis 1 we are introduced to the Holy Spirit that brooded over, or *"covered the waters."* His role in creation was to create an atmosphere where the Word of God could have maximized and marvelous effect. A Christian husband is called the *"head"* of his wife.[1] Scripturally a husband is a spiritual covering for his wife. In the book of Ruth, Naomi tells Ruth to go to Boaz at the threshing floor and ask him to spread his skirt over her.[2] It was to symbolize her coming under his care and protection. In Bible days the Hebraic wedding custom included a robe that the groom placed around the shoulders of his bride to symbolize that she has come under his covenant covering of protection and spiritual, physical, emotional and financial care.

It is important to know that the man himself also must be covered by God! There is this "double layer" that provides all the security, protection, and an atmosphere to flourish in. Men will flourish when they assume this coverer's role in their marriage. It is God's order in marriage for success, happiness and fulfilled living. As coverer, a man provides security, comfort and space for his wife and family. He keeps life's rain out and God's sunlight in. He shields his family by keeping danger out and peace in. He is like the canvas of a tent stretched over a frame to provide essential shelter for his woman. While the Biblical concept of a coverer brings joy, success and fulfillment, there is however also caution -- covering is not smothering! The enemy will try to distort the role of the man in marriage from a coverer to a smotherer. A coverer is sensitive to the needs, desires and passions of the wife and family he covers. Not only does he allow his wife breathing space to express her unique and beautiful attributes, he encourages her to do so. He is firm, yet gentle. A coverer protects but does not isolate, shows his strength as a loving husband, but never in violence, domination or abuse. Just like a greenhouse is an incubator of fruit, the husband is a protector and incubator

---

1 1 Corinthians 11:3-15, Ephesians 5:22-24

2 Ruth 3:9

of the fruits of blessing growing in his wife and family. He is transparent to let the sunlight of God's love shine through him.

Carrier

Women are to be carriers, like a woven basket with a sturdy design and a capacity to carry, enclose and contain the necessities and blessings of life. In fact, women carry and conceal their babies for nine months before giving birth. But God created women to carry more than just children into the world. Remember God created Eve to be a help to Adam, assisting him in all God had appointed him to. As a Carrier, you create comfort, warmth and a loving atmosphere that your husband and children could thrive in by being a nurturer and a nester. Women, you are carriers of dreams, promises and vision of your husband and family. If the husband is the greenhouse then the wife is the good soil in that greenhouse. She is the soil that carries the seed. She nurtures, nourishes and releases the promise of new life. Here too we must issue a caution -- as a carrier a woman must carry what is valuable and treasured. Do not welcome weed-seed into your soil. The enemy will want the carrier to carry the burdens of life; to exchange treasures with troubles. Decide today to carry only what is costly, seed that is guaranteed to produce a harvest of blessing. Carry your coverer's dreams and visions with him. Support him by caring for his heart, passions and joys. We should "Cast our cares on Him (Jesus) because He cares for us."[3] Just like the man is covered by God, the woman is carried by God as well.[4] Again we have here a double layer of purpose. Both coverers and carriers live with purpose and within purpose. It is God's plan for a happy family. Husbands, remember that without your covering your wife's soil will be dried out and unable to carry the seed of success or the fruit of abundance.

As a carrier the women is not to carry out her own agenda and plans but to carry the dreams that are in union with her

---

3 1 Peter 5:17

4 Isaiah 46:4b *"Even I will carry, and will deliver you"*

coverer; and as a coverer the man should not over-power his wife so that she is hidden in obscurity and marginalized.

Think of an old fashioned matchbox. It is really two boxes in one. The outer box covers the inner box, and the inner box carries the matches. Together they form one matchbox. It reminds us of what the Bible says about a husband and wife. They are *"one flesh"*.[5] It takes two to be one. Without the outer box the matches will not be secure in the inner, "carrier" box, and without the inner box the outer box would have nothing to cover. It would be an empty shell. Each box is unique in its own way, but together they are able to fulfill their designed purpose: to carry, protect and light the matches they carry and cover. Men and women need each other. Without his wife, a husband's covering is blemished and without him her carrying is flawed. Together they fulfill God's purposes for parenting. The mother carries, nurtures and cares for her children. The father covers, protects and disciplines them. He lovingly "lights up their bottoms" if they are naughty to correct their behavior.[6] Be the carrier a good coverer would want and be the coverer a good carrier would want. If husbands and wives fulfill their marital roles the best they can, their children will flourish and their household will be a godly unit that functions within divine design and fulfilled purpose.

As a carrier the women is not to carry out her own agenda and plans but to carry the dreams that are in union with her coverer

Remember, a carrier cannot fulfill the role of a coverer and so too a coverer cannot fulfill the role of a carrier. A flipped over basket is not an ideal coverer and a flipped over umbrella is not an ideal carrier. The word "abuse" is derived from "abnormal use". It is important to stay within your assigned role in marriage and not force your spouse into an abnormal

---

5 Genesis 2:24

6 *"Correct your son, and he will give you peace; yes, he will bring delight to your soul."* Proverbs 29:17

function. Using something in any way other than its intended purpose would constitute abuse. For example, if you flip over an open umbrella to carry a bushel of apples the weight will bend the frame and tear the fabric, resulting in an abused umbrella unable to fulfill its original purpose. Likewise, exposing a basket to the elements will corrupt its structure and unravel its fibers, rendering it unable to retain its contents.

What you do to your spouse affects you. Too many couples make each other vulnerable by poking holes into their spouses with the words flowing from their hearts. Wild accusations, criticisms and scorn have no place in a marriage. When you poke holes into your umbrella you are going to get wet. And when you do the same to your basket, be prepared to lose valuables because of the leak you created. So what if I caused a leak in my spouse? It is your responsibility to repair the leak. We have access to God's repair kit that plugs every leak no matter how grave the damage may be. Repentance and forgiveness are two ingredients that when mixed into a situation will create epoxy[7] glue that can repair any marital leak.

As a man or woman you were made to connect to God.

Both umbrellas and baskets have handles. It is important to get a handle on your spouse. How you handle them will determine how your life will be. Lift you man up over you like you would an umbrella to cover you and protect you. Hold onto your wife like you would a basket filled with your personal treasures. Handle each other with dignity, honor and respect. Hold onto them and do not let them go. Let your man be a capital "M" over your life and allow your woman to be a capital "W" underneath you. He will cover and she will carry. He will protect and she will bless. Both handles are in the shape of the letter "J" and stand for

---

7 Epoxy, also known as polyepoxide, is a thermosetting polymer formed from reaction of an exoxide "resin" with polyamine "hardener". Epoxy has a wide range of applications, including fiber-reinforced plastic materials and general purpose adhesives (Wikipedia.com)

Jesus. He is your grip on life. He is the "handle" that upholds both you and your spouse.

Stick to God's plans and purposes. It is important to be what God has made you to be. Men, step up and cover your wife knowing that you yourself are also covered by God. And women support and carry your husband, knowing that you too are carried by the Lord. Being both coverer and carrier at the same time is simply impossible. Each one has its place. When we fulfill our roles there is completeness and harmony in the family structure. Together we can carry, contain, cover and enclose the precious gifts God has blessed us with.

Prayer Application

Dear Heavenly Father
Thank You that You cover and carry me. You have set the standard. Please help me to cover and carry my spouse. Forgive me for shooting holes in my spouse and not realizing the importance of lifting them up. Strengthen my grip to hold onto the blessing You have provided for me in my spouse.
In Jesus Name.
Amen

Notes:

Chapter 3: Faith

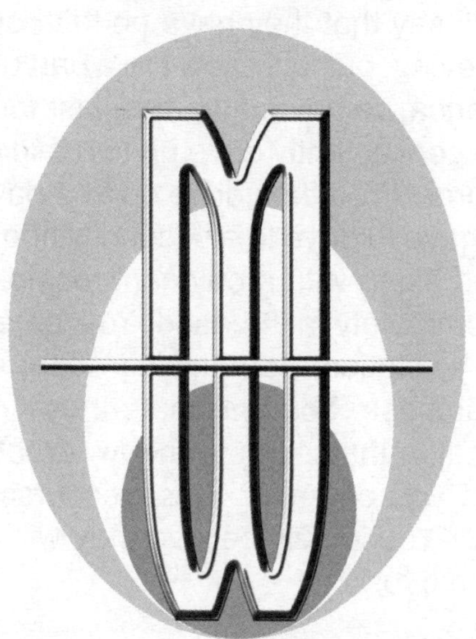

Becoming a Mountain Moving Man And a Wave Walking Woman

Men and women are created to believe. God placed within us a capacity to carry the most important gift He can give you, the gift of faith. Faith connects you to your origin while pointing you to your destiny and it even grounds you in your purpose. *"Without faith it is impossible to please God."*[1] To please God, within scriptural context, means to fully gratify Him; to be fully agreeable and acceptable to Him.[2] Nothing

1 Hebrews 11:6

2 From Strong's Concordance Greek #2101 - "eurestos" - "fully agreeable, acceptable, well-pleasing"

pleases God more than faith. Nothing is more acceptable to Him than your faith in Him.

Some people will say that they have no faith or that they are incapable of believing, but faith-acts are a part of our everyday life. Here in America we have drive-thru fast food restaurants that allow you to conveniently drive up to a microphone-menu and place your order. You then drive up to a payment window and often times have to drive to a second window where you'll receive your food along with a payment receipt. The concept is brilliant and completely faith-based! You leave the payment window without hesitation, not thinking about securing a receipt for your purchase. You anticipate they'll get your order right when you get to the second window. What if they refuse to give you what you ordered? What recourse do you have without a receipt? You simply believe they will give you what you asked and paid for!

We are glad to tell you that faith was not an invention of any fast food restaurant. Faith has its origin in heaven with God. It is God's gift to you to connect you to Him.[3] As a man or woman you were made to connect to God. Faith is the cord that plugs you in to His power and presence.

> *"It is by grace that we are saved through faith, not of ourselves; it is a gift of God."* [4]

Faith is not wishful thinking. It is not a mere positive alternative to a negative mindset that says, "If I hope for it, I might just get what I hope for." Faith is substantive. The Bible says,

> *"Faith is the substance of things hoped for, the evidence of things not seen."* [5]

---

3 Romans 12:3b BBE *"as God has given to everyone a measure of faith"*

4 Ephesians 2:8 NKJV

5 Hebrews 11:1 NKJV

Faith fills hollow hearts with supernatural substance. It provides all the proof you need. It makes you see even that which is invisible and connects you to God's supernatural realm. Faith is a verb and not a noun. Men and women of faith are not hurdled by waves but walk over them and move mountains that hinder their way. What does it mean to be wave walking and mountain moving? It means you are not moved by your circumstances but you change them through active faith. Do not look at the waves. Do not look at the greatness of the mountain. Focus on Jesus. Fix your eyes on Him!

We read in the book of Matthew,

> *"So Jesus answered and said to them, "Assuredly, I say to you, if you have faith and do not doubt, you will not only do what was done to the fig tree, but also if you say to this mountain, 'Be removed and be cast into the sea,' it will be done."* [6]

Faith in Action: Mover

A man who believes in, and speaks the words of God can also speak to the intimidating mountains of circumstances towering over his life. He takes command of the situation. Instead of cursing at an impossible situation he speaks of promise, positivity and possibility, activating his faith by addressing the mountain and letting his words be driven by the force of his faith and not the force of his muscle. Too often men try to move mountains with their muscles. But the Bible says specifically,

> **Mountains can be moved with the help of the Holy Spirit**

> *"Not by might, nor by power, but by My Spirit, says the LORD of hosts. Who are you, Oh great mountain? Before Zerubbabel you shall become*

---

6 Matthew 21:21 NKJV

a plain. . ."[7]

Mountains can be moved with the help of the Holy Spirit. It is a faith thing not a brain thing. A man of faith is a man of prayer. He lives in the authority of God and addresses his circumstances in prayer. He declares, proclaims and enforces the Word and principles of God, drawing confidence and authority from the Lord. He is not intimidated by a problem but addresses it with activated faith, taking authority over it.

Faith in Action: Walker

A woman of faith becomes a wave walker with Jesus. Instead of being swallowed up by waves of circumstance amidst the storms of life, she steps over and not under. Her faith makes her buoyant and unsinkable. She does not drown in circumstances and is not overcome by life's challenges. She fixes her focus on her Savior as Jesus beckons her to join Him on the water. Faith is remarkable! It gives you a reach into the realm of the improbable to pull that what was listed under "impossible" over to the side of the inevitable.

Generally men and women process faith in different ways. For Mountain Moving Men God is the Commander in Chief. He is the general at the top of the chain of command. No matter what position or rank you have attained in life, you are still under the command of God. What He says is. He simply must be obeyed. Faith keeps men in this command structure. It ensures that they will live within the sphere of obedience. A man of faith walks in obedience just like a soldier obeys commands. He becomes task orientated and mission minded. He is on a mission for God. He simply has to protect his family and serve Almighty God. He learns to be a covering for his family because God is his Covering. He respects God and honors His reputation. There is nothing he will not do for His General;

Your faith should always be active and never dormant

7 Zechariah 4:6-7 NKJV

no order is overlooked, challenged or disobeyed.

Wave Walking Women relate to God more in terms of security. God is the great Protector. With His strong hands, God carries her more securely than any vessel on the ocean in a storm. Therefore her faith is an impenetrable shield that keeps her in the safety zone of God's love, even in the midst of harmful debris tossed around her life. No tsunami will wash over her, because her faith in the Wave Walker Himself enables her to walk on the waters of life.

She knows that where He leads He feeds, and where He guides He provides. She is secure in His presence and her faith keeps her there. She is drawn to God's companionship and camaraderie. In Him she has a Listener, a Caregiver, a Protector and a Friend. Being close to Him she thrives and develops confidence and strength, her eyes ever on fixed on Him and not on the waves themselves. Her faith is relational and personal.

On December 9, 1994, the Lord issued me a new order. "Son, work on your English. I am sending you to America." We had been in the ministry for just over 4 years at the time and we were finding our "groove in God" in the city of Bloemfontein, South Africa. We settled into a comfortable stride and saw the Lord touch many lives in our church and city, but the Lord had a new mission for us in a foreign land. I accepted the challenge immediately. The General had spoken. Supply lines would be set up, battle plans drawn up and in God's timing the mission would be a "go". When I shared God's life-altering plans with Sharon, her first response was, "Darling, you can go. I'll pray for you." She was thinking in terms of a short term trip; something like a scouting mission. I realized that it would be unrealistic to expect her to simply activate her faith based on my encounter with God. We would be in it together! Besides, if God gave me the mission-order He could also secure it in Sharon's heart. Sure enough, before long the Lord spoke to Sharon in His own way.

Rudi and I were in a meeting one night and God gave me a powerful vision where we were sitting on two straight back chairs in front of a gigantic American flag. Below this huge flag were many other smaller flags. Then oil, thick as honey, started to flow over the flag from the top down, soaking it. Where the oil flowed, the colors became even more vibrant than before. The oil kept flowing over the flag and then over the two of us. Soaking us, it pooled around the chairs we were sitting on and I watched as from the American flag the oil continued to flow on the flags of the other nations below it. Immediately I knew what the Lord was showing me. He was confirming to me what he already instructed to Rudi. God was sending us to America and from there to other nations we would also go.

Both our faiths were activated concerning this new direction. We were on board with God, agreeing with His plans and purposes for our lives and in harmony with each other every step of the way. We were ready to be mountain moving and wave walking.

Faith will always be tested. It is part of the nature of it. Sometimes men might face stubborn mountains that just won't budge. Women from time to time will face storms that trouble the waves they are supposed to walk on. There might even be moments where it seems as if faith is failing and fear is filling the reservoirs of their hearts. The beauty of true faith is displayed when it is tested. It defies logic and reason and clings relentlessly to Almighty God. It keeps Him in focus amidst trying circumstances.

After months in America we realized that things were not working out the way we planned or the way God had said it would. He promised to open ministry doors for us but none had opened in several months. He said we would travel extensively but it seemed like we were stuck in a "drug-infested" apartment complex in a less than desirable part of town with a car as reliable to leave us stranded on the side of the road as a winter snowstorm in Alaska. In the natural, things were not panning out. Our finances were dwindling and were almost depleted and we became more and more desperate. We prayed, fasted, sighed and struggled and many questions floated to the surface of our hearts. "Were we right in coming to America?" "What if we were not going to make it here?" The enemy even stirred accusations against the Lord. "If God was going to come through for you, He would have done so already." During this challenging season of our lives and ministry we had nothing to hold onto but our faith. We were alone in this and did not look to anybody to bail us out. Neither our family in South Africa or friends knew what we were going through. It was God's word to us and His Spirit dwelling in us that guaranteed our sustenance. Nothing else would stand. All we had was our belief in God and what He said. After all He was Almighty God and in perfect control, even if it felt as if our lives were spinning out of control. He had a reputation that was beyond reproach. He would not leave us nor forsake us.[8] We had history together and because of what we had been through with God in the past made it so much easier to believe Him for the future.

God's Word is the perfect marriage manual, an abundant life guide.

How do you become a man and woman of faith? Well, it is rather simple really -- begin believing. Activate your faith in God. Make a distinction between mere belief and active faith. Let your faith be a verb and not an adjective. Make your faith personal because God is a personal God. Develop a trust in Him that will grow with every encounter with Him. Get to know the Lord, study who He is and what He loves to do and you'll realize who you belong to. Allow the Lord to develop a reputation in your life. Your faith might be fragile at first but

8 According to Hebrews 13:5

with time it will become stronger and stronger. God might not be calling you to a foreign nation as with us, but He has a custom plan for your life. Proving your faith in Him is not always one big leap but a series of small daily steps!

Needless to say, the Lord did come through for us. He allowed us to step out of the season of severe circumstances into more fruitful and desirable times. Doors started to open for us. It did not happen overnight. If we could have it our way we would have accelerated that season of our lives, but looking back today we realize that the Lord used every challenge to strengthen our faith. Mountainous obstacles did move and we learned how to walk on the waves of circumstance together. We discovered that faith should not be reserved for special days or extreme occasions.

Faith should be as common to your soul as food is to your mouth. It should be a way of living; a lifestyle rather than an event. Did you know that life is actually full of faith based actions? You walk into a dark room and flick a switch in anticipation of light. You do this without thinking, praying or hesitation. You anticipate that electricity will flow through the circuit to the light bulb that will in turn illuminate your room. You are acting in faith, reinforced by previous experience. Most people cannot describe the complex processes of the flow of electricity from the moment you "flick the switch" to when you see the light. They simply know it works. They act in faith without even thinking about it. Faith can become second nature if you choose to live a life of faith.

Faith should be as common to your soul as food is to your mouth

Your faith should always be active and never dormant,

> *"For as the body without the spirit is dead, so faith without works is dead."* [9]

9 James 2:26 NKJV

Your faith anchors you to God while fear glues you to your circumstances. Faith does not guarantee visual impulse. It is often blind to visual aid but it does promise you eventual victory. It provides evidence into what had been invisible and unseen before, resulting in a settled spirit and a reassured soul. It lifts you up over life's waves and causes landscapes of life to change and mountainous challenges to be moved.

Do not allow your circumstances to be a challenge to you. Rather be challenged today to be a wave walker and a mountain mover. We challenge you to activate that precious measure of faith that God has given to you.[10]

Two are better than one

> *"Two people are better off than one, because they can help each other succeed."* [11]

This statement is especially true in marriage. Men, you do not have to stand before the mountain alone. Look, beside you is the life mate God gave you. And if you look on your other side you'll see the Helper Himself ready to strengthen you and act on your faith. Women, you do not have to walk on the waves amidst stormy life conditions alone. Beside you is your appointed faith partner and on your other side your Senior Partner, the Holy Spirit, who will direct your steps as you walk in the Spirit.

---

10 Romans 12:3
11 Ecclesiastes 4:9 NLT

Prayer Application

Dear Heavenly Father
Please help me to have my eyes opened and my faith activated, by Your Word, being made able to walk on waves and move mountains of opposition in my life. You have spoken and said, "Come, walk with me, and speak to the mountains." Thank you for giving me the ability to change landscapes and experience the supernatural in You. I will follow You.
In Jesus Name.
Amen.

Notes:

Chapter 4: Character

Men of Message
And
Women of the Word

The world needs men and women of character. People who know who they are, recognize right and wrong, and decide to live their lives in the right and not the wrong, to walk in the truth even when the truth is inconvenient, and to stand strong when others are failing and falling.

But what exactly is character? How do I get it? Can I measure its fortitude? Here are a few synonyms for the word character: "nature, quality, temperament, moral fiber, disposition, spirit, make-up." Your character is the framework that carries your image, reputation, gifts, abilities, emotions, and principles. It defines you. It is the rebar that keeps you upright even amidst life's tornado winds. It is what is left when all else is stripped away. It determines how you make decisions. It tells you how to act and respond. It controls your emotions and keeps them in check. A good character is not bought, borrowed or inherited. It is fashioned and developed in your spirit over the course of your life. A strong moral fiber already made the tough choices for you. It sets the baseline of boundaries you are unwilling to cross no matter what. It frees you to live life to the fullest within the boundaries your character will allow. Character is not legalistic, it is principled. It is not negative but wonderfully positive. While legalism steers you away from things, principles point you towards what's right.

Just like the construction of any strong building, the formation of your character starts with a solid foundation. Your character/framework must rest on a secure foundation. Jesus said,

> *"Therefore whoever hears these sayings of Mine, and does them, I will liken him to a wise man who built his house on a rock. And the rain came down, and the floods came, and the winds blew and beat on that house. And it did not fall, for it was founded on a rock."*[1]

Remember, your character will only be as strong as the foundation it rests on. There is no sounder, more solid and stable foundation than the Word of God. Living your life within the framework of God's Word will ensure your character to develop in a divine way. It will stand through every test, challenge and guide you through every decision you will make.

---

1 Matthew 7:24-25 NKJV

Build your house on the Rock. Jesus is the Rock[2] and He is the Word.[3]

The Bible is a light unto the path of men and women alike.[4] God is not a chauvinist or a feminist. He is not a respecter of persons.[5] He does not choose sides. We are the ones that need to choose: His side or our side, His way or ours. God's Word is the perfect marriage manual, an abundant life guide. It is God's inspired will for both men and women. Knowing His Word secures your life by planting you in fertile yet stable ground. The seed contained in His Word will sprout and grow in your soul and your once barren landscape will become a lush garden retreat. God has a "can do" word for you every day.

Men of the Message

The Bible is not for sissies. It is God's Word and contains God's inspired will for our lives. Bible believing men dare to stand for something that is bigger than themselves. They are principled and disciplined. Men of the Message have chosen to depend on the development of a good and strong character; one that will not allow them to be swayed by emotions or influenced through peer pressure. Their focus is to pursue God's will for their lives and families. Such men are true mountain movers. They are not ashamed of the Gospel of Christ because it is the power of God unto salvation to everyone who believes.[6] Because they do not cater to their own fleshly will they allow God's Word to shape them as they apply the various disciplines of God's

God's Word is more than theory or theology. It is practical, powerful and persuasive.

2 Acts 4:11 NKJV "*This is the Stone which you builders have counted worthless, and He has become the Head of the Corner.*"

3 John 1:1, 14 *"In the beginning was the Word. . . and the Word became flesh and dwelt among us. . ."*

4 Psalm 119:105

5 Acts 10:34

6 Romans 1:16

Word to their lives.

They are men of influence because they have been influenced by God's Word. Their words, actions, emotions, and conduct become a message board to display the glory of God to those around them. Paul said,

> *"You are clearly a letter of Christ, the fruit of our work, recorded not in ink, but with the Spirit of the living God; not in stone, but in hearts of flesh."* [7]

Mountain Moving Men are not men of their own message but have welcomed and embraced the glorious gospel message of Jesus Christ. Their lives are also a bill board filled with messages read by the people they interact with. Men of Message most often become mentors to others who need structure and strengthening in their own characters. Are you a Man of the Message? What is the message that your life displays to your family?

> **As you weave your life around the Word of God the fiber of your character will be unbreakable. It will stand the test of time.**

The concept of Men of Message incorporates the message of God's Word into every area of their lives and their families are the true beneficiaries of these men's characters. They are good, loving husbands. Actions speak louder than words and Men of Message lead by example. Their lives are a message that will influence, shape, and in many ways determine the destiny of their loved ones. Aspiring to correct past mistakes, eliminating current destructive issues and preventing future personal mishaps, they are realistic enough to know that life is both bitter and sweet, allowing the message of God's Word to influence how they deal with both. They're strong in the storms, fierce in defending their family from evil

7 2 Corinthians 3:3

attacks, gentle in dealing with those they love and devoted to *"the Author and Finisher of their faith"*.[8]

They do not carry their own message or revelation, but live the victorious and glorious message of the cross. They carry a word of authority and power in their mouths. Men, let us be men of message and substance. Let's be selfless and not selfish and love our wives as God loves us.

Women of the Word

The Bible is prominent in the hearts of Wave Walking Women. God's Word is always on their lips. They are encouragers that reinforce others as they share the powerful principles of the Word of God. Such women are not preachy but do not shy away from dynamic declarations that confirm the will of God in any given situation. Their opinions are coveted and celebrated by their friends. Women of the Word have their feet planted firmly on the Word of God. God's words in the mouths of both men of message and women of the Word, are as powerful as God's words in His mouth. Women of the Word build, encourage, lead and affirm truth with their tongues. After all, death and life are in the power of the tongue and they that love it shall eat the fruit thereof.[9] Their positive words bring death to negativity. Faith echoes from their mouths and allows potential to come alive and be realized according to God's wondrous purposes and plans. Because they allow God's Word to guide them, they too become life-leaders who impact those around them. They do not judge others or throw around wild accusations, but live the Word. And understand that the Word is not merely guidelines and instructions written on paper but in reality the Person of Jesus Christ.[10] As a matter of fact, Women of the Word and Men of the Message are filled with grace and compassion for others and not judgment and

---

8 Hebrews 12:2

9 Proverbs 18:21

10 John 1:1 *"In the beginning was the Word and the Word was with God and the Word was God."*

condemnation. God's Word to them is more than theory or theology. It is practical, powerful and persuasive.

Women of the Word put their families second only to God in their lives. They are loving, dedicated wives to their husbands and mothers to their children. Let's look again at Ephesians,

> *"Wives, understand and support your husbands in ways that show your support for Christ. The husband provides leadership to his wife the way Christ does to His church, not by domineering but by cherishing. So, just as the church submits to Christ as He exercises such leadership, wives should likewise submit to their husbands"*[11]

"Submission" here is not a sign of weakness or inferiority; on the contrary, it shows remarkable strength and character to follow God's principles for a healthy and strong marriage. Women of the Word obey the Word. They support and help their husbands to the best of their ability. They enhance, give aid and make their spouses look and feel good. Behind every flourishing husband is a loving, encouraging and motivating wife. They use not their own words but God's words in their mouths.[12] They build up, care for and encourage. Their own opinions are always secondary to the Word of God. They carry God's message both in words and deeds. They do what they say and say what they do. Gossip, bragging and nagging should not flow from their mouths. They know the difference between smothering and mothering. Theirs is a warm blanket of love to their family and not a wet blanket of regret and accusation. They nurture, support, instruct and defend their children like a lioness her cubs.

Building Strong Character

---

11 5:22-24 The Message (Emphasis Added)

12 Proverbs 27:15 NLT *"A quarrelsome wife is as annoying as constant dripping on a rainy day."*

So how do we keep our character strong? Stay in the Word. It is not enough to rely on yesterday's knowledge of God's Word. We must keep our lives polished by the Word. The Bible reminds us,

> *"Husbands, love your wives, even as Christ also loved the church, and gave Himself for it; that He might sanctify and cleanse it with the washing of water by the Word, that He might present it to Himself as the glorious church, without spot or wrinkle, or any such things, but that it would be holy and without blemish."* [13]

The church He is referring to here is not the building in which we gather to worship. It is not the institution with its hierarchies. The church is Christ's followers, men and women, who connected with God through their faith and live their lives in obedience to the One who saved and set them free from sin and shame. Jesus so loved His church that He gave Himself for us! Why would He do that? We were not "lovable material". He wanted to sanctify and cleanse our lives through the washing of water by the Word.

It is not enough to rely on yesterday's knowledge of God's Word. We must keep our lives polished by the Word.

Men of the message and women of the Word are holy, their characters cleansed, their souls sanctified and their lives consecrated to Almighty God. The washing of water by the Word is a daily thing much like our daily hair-, teeth-, and body-cleansing routines. Neglect your teeth and cavities appear, refuse to wash your body and dirt and grime allows infectious bacteria to enter your body. God's applied word everyday keeps sin and temptations away.

So men, what is your message to your coworkers, your family,

13 Ephesians 5:25-27 NKJV

your God and yourself? Is it a message of hope and destiny or defeat and destruction? When people read your actions and listen to your words will they be encouraged and strengthened or shocked and repulsed? Are you laying a foundation for a lasting legacy or will you be forgotten even before you departed? Is your character strong as a fortress or flimsy and weak?

Women, on whose words are you building your life? Is it some fashionable celebrity that is out to please and not offend? Do you believe past lies spoken over you that were designed to hurt your heart and destroy your confidence? Are you constantly trying to defend yourself and your own opinions? What words are flowing from your mouth? Are you using your words to cut or to build?

Watch your thoughts, they become words,
Watch your words, they become actions
Watch your actions, they become habits and
Your habits define your character [14]

As you weave your life around the Word of God the fiber of your character will be unbreakable. It will stand the test of time. Jesus said,

> "Sky and earth will pass away, but My words will not pass away." [15]

Being a Man of the Message and a Woman of the Word will ensure a lasting legacy that will point your children and loved ones in God's direction and encourage them to pursue all that Heaven has for them.

---

14 Unknown
15 Matthew 24:35 AMP.

Prayer Application

Dear Heavenly Father
May Your Word be alive in me and may the message I bring to others be one of victory. Lord Your Word is life-giving, so let the message of my life reflect Your life. Please help me to show your Gospel message to all. Guard my mouth so that I will not judge others but declare life in a situation of death, healing in a situation of sickness and hope in despair.
In Jesus Name.
Amen.

Notes:

Chapter 5: Worship

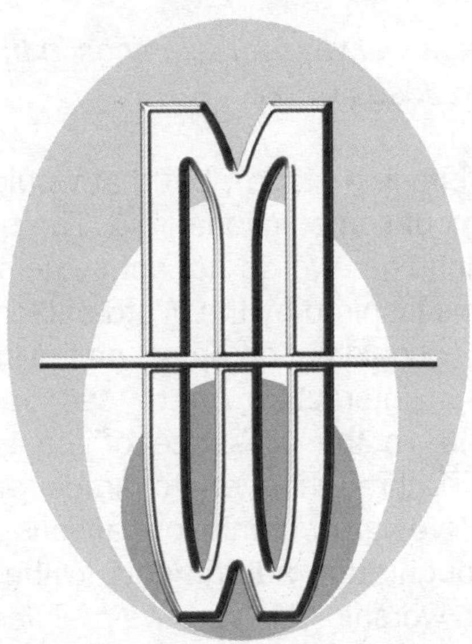

Meditating Men And Waiting Women

Worship is central in the life of a believer. The reality of God ensures the validity of worship. If our God was a dead statue or a mere image on a piece of paper, our worship would be equally dead and worthless. People who worship statues, in meditation their posture mimic the lifeless gods they serve. But because our God is the Almighty, living Creator of heaven and earth, our worship reflects His life and vibrancy. When we speak about worship we are not referring to a mere activity or ritual. Worship is so much more than that. So what is true worship?

Worship is first and foremost a lifestyle. Every action, word, step and motive of our hearts point to worship. The Bible says,

> *"Giving thanks always for all things in the name of our Lord Jesus Christ."* [1]

Someone said, "Life is a stage", but that would simply make us actors playing out some fictional role. The believer's life is not an act, it is genuine. We do not act as actors pretending, we act with actions inspired by the Word of God. Although we could put on an act on the stage of human interaction, there can be no pretense in the presence of the Lord. He sees through every charade and caricature. As a believer our lives are worship, our actions are adorations and even our thoughts are adornments to the glory of God. We were made to worship. It is who we are! Jesus declared,

Begin and end your day with Him.

> *"But the hour is coming, and now is, when the true worshipers will worship the Father in spirit and truth; for the Father is seeking such to worship Him."* [2]

True worshippers worship God in spirit and truth. Their worship is not based on mere ritual or fleshly routine. Worship that comes from the depth of your spirit, which is stirred with the passion of your soul and carried on the genuineness of your heart, is true worship. The opposite of spirit and truth is flesh and lies. The Pharisees were masters at the art of false worship. Their worship was offered always in public places to impress as many people as possible. They would use pomp and public piety to play on the passions of the people.[3]

---

1 Ephesians 5:20 ASV

2 John 4:23 NKJV

3 Matthew 6:5 NLT *"When you pray, don't be like the hypocrites who love to pray publicly on street corners and in the synagogues where everyone can see them. I tell you the truth, that is all the reward they will*

Why worship?

Worship is not for God's benefit. Nothing we say can make God bigger and better than He already is. No amount of glory we ascribe to Him can make Him more glorious. Our accolades and honor we bestow on Him does not give Him a higher stance or purer persona. He is God already and He fully earned that title. He is unimprovable because He is perfect in every way. He already functions at the optimum level all the time.

Our worship changes us! When we tell Him how great He is it reminds us how great He is. When we ascribe glory to Him it reminds us of the immense glory He has. When we sing about His love it reminds us of His amazing love. Do you get it? Worship is important because it keeps our focus on who God is. It fixes our attention on the solution rather than our problems, on our Redeemer rather than our sin, and on our blessed future with Him rather than our disappointing past in the clutches of the enemy.

Waiting and Meditating

Waiting and meditating is about taking time to spend in the presence of God. Push distractions aside. Both men and women should wait on God and meditate on His Word. When we speak of Waiting Women, we also include men and when we speak of Meditating Men we include women.

Waiting Women know the value of patient anticipation in adoration. Their hearts are settled on the One who saved them. They are not pressured to act on impulse or to follow the newest cultural whim simply to fit in. They rest in the presence of Almighty God. They move when He moves them and they respond to His desires and are stirred by His Holy Spirit. They make a point to wait on the Lord. This waiting is not a passive, impatient wait as if you are waiting on a train or a bus. The

---

ever get."

Bible declares,

> *"But those who wait on the LORD shall renew their strength; They shall mount up with wings like eagles, They shall run and not be weary, They shall walk and not faint."* [4]

The Hebrew word for *"wait"* here means *"to wait; to look eagerly for; or to hope."* [5] Waiting Women worship with eagerness and hope. Their expectation is on the Lord and their worship activates spiritual strength, life-stamina, and patient endurance. While spending time in God's presence, they are elevated above circumstances and situations. They ride on the winds of the Holy Spirit. Waiting Women wait not in their problems and circumstances until God comes to the rescue. They wait in God as He lifts them up and out.

Our worship changes us! When we tell Him how great He is it reminds us how great He is.

In America, dining out is part of the lifestyle. Usually any type of celebration includes food and often in some restaurant. A good waiter or waitress is very valuable to an eating establishment. Good service is almost just as important to the patrons as good food. Good waiters are attentive, courteous and fast. They make each table feel as if they are the most important in the whole restaurant. They will frequent the table to check on the guests and often anticipate what guests might need. In worship, we wait on the Lord! He is our VIP guest and we are ready to wait on Him according to His desires. We wait on Him because we love Him. Worship is our one chance to be a blessing to our Creator, to please Him in ways that will put a smile on His face and stir warmth in His heart, to lavish love on Him in moments that you do not expect anything in return. Keep in mind God is a great tipper! Good waiters can expect good tips. Oftentimes

4 Isaiah 40:31 NKJV

5 Strong's Concordance Hebrew #6960

stories surface of some waiter receiving a tip worth more than the meal itself! One waitress mentioned to her table that her child would love to go to college and by the end of the meal a guest arranged for an education trust fund to pay for such an endeavor! As waiters in worship we wait on the Almighty God.

We find wonderful examples of a waiting woman in the Bible. Mary waited at the feet of Jesus. She took a pound of ointment of spikenard, a very costly perfume and anointed the feet of Jesus. The fragrance of her worship filled the whole house they were in.[6] Not only did she spend time at the feet of Jesus, she worshipped sacrificially. That perfume cost about a year's wages for an average worker. Her worship was costly and pure, exclusive and expensive. She would sacrifice anything to honor Him. She would stop at nothing to bring glory to Jesus.

During our engagement we lived between three and four hours apart. I would visit Sharon on the weekends at her parent's house. Every Friday afternoon Sharon would be waiting for the arrival of her sweetheart. She would be ready well in advance of my arrival and would alternate between the mirror in her room and the little window through which she could monitor the driveway outside. Her excitement and anticipation was legendary and had the whole house on alert. Her family would enjoy her passionate waiting almost as much as I enjoyed seeing her run across the lawn to meet me the moment I arrived at her house. Waiting Women are electrifying. Their worship will put others on the edge of anticipation as well, looking for and waiting for the moment in worship that the Prince of Peace enters their existence in all His glory. Their "red carpet treatment" of God in their devotion to Him will bless and inspire many. They are blessed with lavish "tips of blessings" from the hands of God.

Meditating Men fill their minds with the Word and wonder of

---

6 John 12:3

God. They bring God into every situation. The Bible says,

> *"And do not be conformed to this world, but be transformed by the renewing of your mind, that you may prove what is that good and acceptable and perfect will of God."* [7]

Biblical meditation is the opposite of what new age followers and eastern religions teach. Instead of emptying your mind and spirit of everything to discover self, believers meditate on the Word of God. They fill their minds and hearts with the inspired teachings of God and discover who He really is and what He made them to be.

It reminds us of our espresso maker at home. To make a good cup of coffee you have to fill the basket with your favorite coffee and tamp (stamp) it in. The problem is that after you make your coffee you have to clean the basket. We found that an easy way to clean it is to put the basket under a flowing faucet. The clean water flows into the basket and loosens the old coffee grounds. It is messy at first, but the longer you keep it under the water, the cleaner your basket will be. Soon the clean water will have displaced the old, brown coffee grounds. We are all guilty of stinking thinking. Our understanding is limited in so many areas and our thoughts crooked in so many ways, especially when it comes to the virtues of life, the importance of godly character and the power of integrity. We often fill our mind-baskets full of old, outdated and stale coffee ground thoughts. We need our minds to be washed, renewed and renovated.

Meditating Men know where the living water flows. They position their lives in worship under the spout where the living water comes out. They know that if they get more of God's Word into their lives their actions will be purer, their walk stronger and their commitment to God unending. Worship is for war-

---

7 Romans 12:2 NKJV

riors. David was a warrior. He grabbed a lion by the beard and then killed it. Yet he was a man who was a worshipper of God. Both privately and publicly he did not hesitate to bring his devotion to the Lord. He was as passionate in worship as he was in war. Whether he fought the giants of life or worshiped God he gave 100% of himself. He did not hold back. Worship made his heart pure and gave his spirit depth. When we read the Psalms he wrote we are struck with his amazing understanding and perspective of life.

Meditating Men are not shallow. Through an attitude of worship they gain divine understanding into the complexities of life. They are able to bring a fresh perspective into old mindsets, stale methods and sinful memories. Meditating Men are ministering men and vice versa. They are ready to serve and to minister.

Worship is for warriors

How to Worship

Lifestyle worship is our primary mode of worship simply because it is our continual, nonstop worship service to Almighty God. But we have to secure specific times of dedicated worship to the Lord. Both private and public worship is very important in the lives of believers. In private worship you are spending personal times with God. He stirs a personal anointing that shapes your soul for everyday living. In corporate worship the dynamics change. You join fellow believers in worship, being led into the presence of the Lord. There is a valuable and irreplaceable corporate anointing that flows during such times. The Bible speaks of the importance of both types of worship.[8] Christians are often charged with being hypocrites by nonbelievers. They oftentimes hear us say one thing and act in an opposite way. Worship will help to keep us genuine and true to the teachings of God. Our private worship should not be different than our public worship. When we sing, we sing to an audience of One. When we pray, we pray to an audience of One,

8 Hebrews 10:25 and Psalm 63:1-2

regardless of the venue or a sizable attendance. This was often our litmus test for those who wanted to join the worship team in our church. If they worshiped in the pews regardless of being on the platform, then we knew they would worship on the platform regardless of who is sitting in the pews.

As Meditating Men and Waiting Women we should take time in every day to worship the Lord. We should wait on Him and meditate on His Word. We should practice holiness 24/7. We should bring Him into our lives at church, at work, at home, and everywhere.

Begin and end your day with Him. Make time to read His Word. A great habit is to commit to a Bible reading schedule that will let you read the entire Bible through in one year. This will take about 15 minutes a day. Another way to bring the Lord into your day is to listen to praise and worship music. In fact, you can fill your home with the sound of praise and worship music 24/7. You'll be amazed at how it will change the atmosphere of your house. People will soon comment on it.

We place a very high priority on praise and worship in our meetings. Wherever we go we dedicate a portion of the meeting to leading God's people into deep intimate worship. We have a mandate from the Lord to usher in His glory wherever we go. We have found worship to be the best way to usher in His glory. What we also discovered is that it does not just work in church gatherings, but also privately when you are alone with the Lord. A few moments in God's presence will clear your head, calm your spirit and prepare your heart for whatever challenge you may face. God's omnipresence is one of the His glorious facets. He is not just waiting for us in the sanctuary of our churches on Sunday morning to be worshipped. We can worship Him anywhere all

Worship changes your concept of things. It points you upwards and focuses your attention on God and not on self or circumstances.

the time.

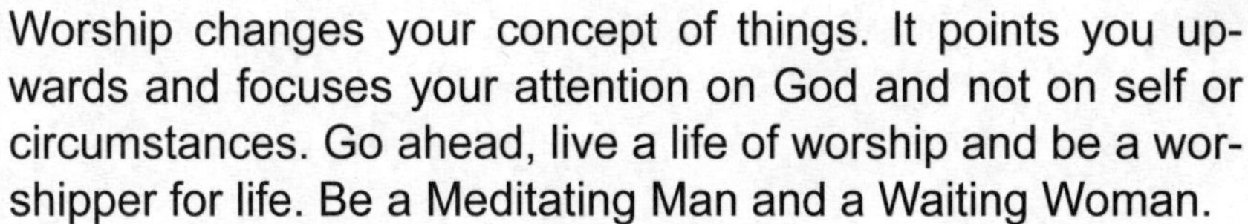

Worship changes your concept of things. It points you upwards and focuses your attention on God and not on self or circumstances. Go ahead, live a life of worship and be a worshipper for life. Be a Meditating Man and a Waiting Woman.

Prayer Application

Dear Heavenly Father
Thank you for making Yourself known to me in such a special way. I worship you Almighty God, Creator of heaven and earth. Help me to fill my mind with Your Word and my life with Your presence. As I wait on You today, cause me to mount up on wings like eagles, to run and not grow weary, to walk and not faint.
In Jesus name.
Amen.

Notes:

Chapter 6: Relationship

Marrying Men And Wedding Women

Marriage is a God idea and not merely a good idea. It is not something humans came up with. It is not merely a ceremony where we celebrate our mutual love with a big party. Marriage existed long before any state sanctioned it. We do not get married because it is economical or even logical. We marry because it is a God-thing to do.

Yes, marriage originated with God. He established it to create an ideal environment for men and women to flourish in together. And because God packaged it we need to know His thoughts, principles and purposes for marriage before we add our own two cents to it. In marriage men and women can find a perfect place to fully become what God intended them to be.

Origins

God consummated the first marriage in the Garden of Eden. He brought Adam and Eve together after He created them.

> *"Then the Lord caused Adam to sleep and he fashioned a woman from one of Adam's ribs, and God "brought her unto the man."* [1]

Adam immediately responded. He exclaimed,

> *"This is now bone of my bones, and flesh of my flesh: she shall be called Woman, because she was taken out of Man. Therefore shall a man leave his father and his mother, and shall cleave unto his wife: and they shall be one flesh."* [2]

Because of Adam's declaration this phrase "bone of my bones and flesh of my flesh" was used in Bible times when people made a covenant with each other. It was the strongest language that showed lifelong intent. These words were an expression of a binding agreement or covenant that could not be retracted or negated. A good example of this was when the people of Israel came to David in Hebron and said,

Marriage is a covenant between a man and a woman

> *"Indeed we are your bone and your flesh."* [3]

1 Genesis 2:22 KJV
2 Genesis 2:23-24 KJV
3 1 Chronicles 11:1 NKJV

They went on to cut a covenant with David and made him king over all of Israel. Even Jesus, when he taught the people while ministering on earth acknowledged the institution of marriage,

> *"And He answered and said to them, "Have you not read that He who made [them] at the beginning made them male and female, and said, 'For this reason a man shall leave his father and mother and be joined to his wife, and the two shall become one flesh'? So then, they are no longer two but one flesh. Therefore what God has joined together, let not man separate"* [4]

Marriage is a covenant between a man and a woman. Scripturally there is no such thing as same-sex marriage. It is an invention of man and not sanctioned anywhere in God's Word. God's original intent for marriage was with a man and a women and that has not changed. In the Bible marriage is recorded as the first covenant ever made. This covenant is a life-long commitment and not a temporary arrangement. It is sacred because it originates with, and is sanctioned by God. The vows of marriage are not just nice words you exchange to "seal the deal". They are the expression of a covenant made between husband and wife, "'till death do us part". In marriage there is no room for "falling out of love." Our love is secured by the covenant we made with each other. It matures into the highest expression of honor, devotion and respect. Marriage was designed to last for life.

Almighty God does not do anything without purpose and one of the sacred reasons He instituted marriage was to give us a glimpse into His covenant relationship with saved humanity.

> *"The husband is head of the wife, as also Christ is head of the church; and He is the Savior of*

4 Matthew 19:4-6 NKJV

the body." [5]

The relationship between husband and wife is compared to the intended relationship between Christ and the church. In fact the church is also referred to as the bride of Christ. God did not create us for His amusement. He made us to be His companions, and His soul mates. His love for us runs deeper than what we can understand. He brought us to Himself and signed an eternal covenant in His own blood to care for, support and love us.

Marrying Men

The Word of God is clear,

> *"He who finds a wife finds a good thing, and obtains favor from the Lord."* [6]

The word for *"find"* in this verse literally means *"to find, secure, acquire, get (thing sought)"*[7] If a man is ready to get married, he should rely on God to bring the right wife to him. We believe there is a proper lid for every pot in this world. Someone special God made just for you! We always say that when Sharon was born God had Rudi on His mind and when Rudi was born God thought of Sharon.

> *"If you seek, you will find."* [8]

Let your search start with a declaration of faith that the Lord will bring her to you. If you are married already then believe and apply this verse -- that He brought her to you already and that in your wife you have found a good thing and obtained favor from the Lord. The Hebrew word for *"good thing"* here means *"benefit, happiness, welfare, prosperity"*. God

---

5 Ephesians 5:23 NKJV
6 Proverbs 18:22 NKJV
7 Strong's Concordance Hebrew #4672 - "matsa"
8 Matthew 7:7

was good to you in giving you such a wife! He prospered and favored you. You are truly blessed! When we, husbands and wives, allow the Lord to shape us then we all become better than we were before. Everything God made is indeed good.

You have a specific role within your marriage. When you do your part it allows your wife to flourish and be the blessing to you that God intended. Before you can accuse your wife of not being a blessing or failing to be that *"good thing"* the Bible speaks of, you must be sure to fulfill your designated role in your marriage. Remember the old saying: "It takes two to tango."

We already saw in chapter 2 that the man is a coverer. Let's look at the Biblical terms that describe a man's intended function within a marriage. The husband is the head of the wife just like Christ is the head of the church. If we as men want to know what it means to be the head of the house, we need to look at how Christ is head of the church. His position is identified in love. When you think of Jesus you think of love first. He gave His life for humanity. As husbands we need to love our wives in the same way. We need to step it up, don't you think? Women respond to love. They were made that way. The more you love her, the greater blessing she'll be to you. One day a married couple came up to Sharon at a meeting in a church. The husband jokingly said, "You are so beautiful. I remember when my wife was as beautiful as you. When I married her she was a beautiful rose, but now she is an old cactus." Sharon was stunned, but without skipping a beat she looked him in the eye and said, "Sir, why have you stopped giving her water?" Her point was clear. If the man continued to water his wife in the way a rose needs watering, then she would have never evolved to the life of a cactus in a loveless marital desert.

You are not called to be a dominating dictator. You are called to be loving husband

As head of his wife, every husband needs to step into the role of protector. Remember you are to cover her and not smother her. She needs to feel safe and secure. If you are able to create an atmosphere of safety around her, she will flourish. How can men accomplish this? By mimicking what God does in the life of a believer. In fact, believers should have an edge in marriage over non-believers. As you experience God in a personal relationship and encounter His love, support and attention first hand in your life, you'll know how to pour the same into the precious wife the Lord gave you. Be the greenhouse for her to flourish in.

Being the head of your wife is not about position but function and purpose. You are not called to be a dominating dictator. You are called to be loving husband.

> *"Husbands, love your wives, just as Christ also loved the church and gave Himself for her."* [9]

Give her your love and you'll get it back many times over! Maybe you are thinking, "How can my love be compared to God's love?" After all who can compete with Divine love? Well, we believe love is truly a gift from God. The Bible says, *"God is love."*[10] God also, *"gave Himself to us."*[11] If then you have received the Gift of love, let Him flow through you to your wife and family. Here is another way to look at it,

A personal relationship with Christ is not only important, but essential for you to lead your wife spiritually.

> *"So husbands ought to love their own wives as their own bodies; he who loves his wife loves himself."* [12]

---

9 Ephesians 5:25 NKJV
10 1 John 4:8
11 John 3:16
12 Ephesians 5:28 NKJV

You can never place yourself above your wife. You must love her in the same way you love yourself. She is part of you! When you love her you love yourself and when you love yourself, you can love her like you should. Think about it. God loved you so much that Jesus stepped into your shoes, became your sin and died your death so you might live His kind of life and enjoy heaven with Him forever. You did not do anything to deserve His love, He simply gave it. And as you accept His love you are changed by His love never to be the same again. Now decide to love your wife like that! Not because of what she does for and to you, not according to the level of love she deserves and certainly not because she loves you. Simply love her for being your wife; for being the "good thing" you found and because you obtained favor from God. Without your love she can never be complete as your wife. You two belong together and together you belong to God.

King, Priest and Prophet

Scripturally your must fulfill three primary roles in marriage. It is who the Lord made you to be. First you are king. You rule the roost. Any king can either be a good king or a bad king. Choose to be a good one today! A good king protects, feeds, and loves his subjects. He does not see them as his possessions but as his treasures. He knows that a king without subjects is no king at all. With his wealth he provides infrastructure to his kingdom and with his army he defends and protects. He rules with his wisdom and is the visible authority that keeps outlaws in check.

You are a king to your wife and home. Remember, Jesus is the King of kings and in scripture your marital role to your wife is compared to Christ's role to the church. He is the best King and you can and should learn from Him. You can be a great king too. As king you should establish a safe "palace" for your wife to flourish in. You should keep her secure physically, mentally and spiritually.

Secondly, you are called to be the priest of your household. Not only is Jesus King, He is also our High Priest. He provides spiritual leadership and guidance. He points to God with His actions and leads us to the Father. Scripture says that,

> *"No one comes to the Father except through Him."* [13]

That is a huge responsibility. If He does his job well, and He always does, then we can get to know the Father personally and intimately.

As priest, you too should point your loved ones towards and not away from God. Your actions should gravitate towards Him. If your wife follows your spiritual guidance will she get to know God personally and intimately? If not, then you are not the priest you could and should be. You are the pastor of your home. Pastors do much more than just preach. You should love and lead your wife. You should show her that actions speak louder than words; that your sermons are all illustrated by the life you live both publicly and privately. You should take her to church. You should lead her spiritually. You should read the Bible to her and pray with her. You should establish devotions together. Come on, be the priest! Your family's spiritual growth is in your hands. Their spiritual potential will amaze you. It is never too late to start. A true priest is not someone who merely gives directions. He is not the good guy on the sidewalk giving direction towards a destination. He is more like a GPS system in a car. He gives direction in real time. He moves with his family towards their spiritual destination.

Before you can be priest of your house, you must know the One you serve. A personal relationship with Christ is not only important, but essential for you to lead your wife spiritually. Far too many husbands are absent in this respect, or they are spiritually lost themselves. You simply must get your bearing.

---

13 John 14:6b

Find your place in the presence of the Lord. Locate God's will and destiny for your family and lead them to that marvelous place. Just like a GPS that stays in constant communication with several satellites to stay accurate and on course, you should maintain close contact with the Word of God and the leading of the Holy Spirit. He wants to guide you much more than you want to be led.

Thirdly, you are called the prophet of your household. A prophet in Bible times was a messenger of God. He would send prophets with "Thus says the Lord. . ." - Messages. They revealed the will of God to others. Their words came from the Lord and when they spoke their messages transformed lives and penetrated spirits. Many times the prophets pointed to the future and boldly declared what the Lord had shown them. They were able to see things before they happened. They would find answers when people brought questions and kept their eyes and ears tuned in to hear what God's will was for a specific situation.

You too need to hear from heaven. As husband you need to provide direction and leadership but also divine council. You too can get a "This is what God spoke to me. . ." - Word.

The wealth of a man is not measured in his wallet, but in his wife!

A family can flourish when the king, priest and prophet is on duty. When you lead your family through God's will and not man's directives; when you keep their lives revolving around Him and not their own selfish agendas or even around you. Today I posted on Facebook something the Lord stirred in my heart: "When life starts to revolve around you, maybe it is time to get a bigger bowl. Even gold fish can be big in a small bowl. Better yet, jump into the ocean for a true perspective on life. Our hearts should outgrow our heads." It is your duty as husband and head of your household to keep their heads in heaven and their feet on the ground, to absorb God's Word and reflect His glory and splendor. To share His love and glorious message of forgiveness and salvation in everything they do and say. They will follow your lead and example. They'll start to do what you do, say what you say and be who you are.

We love the verses in Ephesians,

> *"The husband provides leadership to his wife the way Christ does to His church, not by domineering but by cherishing. Husbands, go all out in your love for your wives, exactly as Christ did for the church – a love marked by giving, not getting. Christ's love makes the church whole. His words evoke her beauty. Everything He does and says is designed to bring the best out of her, dressing her in dazzling white silk, radiant with holiness. And that is how husbands ought to love their wives. They're really doing themselves a favor – since they're already "one" in marriage."* [14]

To God, men are not more important than women. There should be no competition among the sexes. Both men and women have extremely powerful and important roles to play in building a strong, and flourishing family life together.

You do not have to be the perfect king, priest or prophet. A king does not abdicate his throne every time he makes a mistake. A priest does not turn his back on his calling when he messes up. A prophet does not throw in the towel when he feels defeat. David was a great king, Aaron was a tremendous high priest and Elijah was a potent prophet, yet all three of them made mistakes. They became great in spite of their sin because they stayed with God and true to their call in life. The enemy wants you to step down from what God has called you to step up to. Your weaknesses are no excuse for you to opt out of God's design for your life.

---

14 Ephesians 5:23, 25-28 The Message

Marrying Men cover their wives with love and security. They care for and respect their spouses and treat them with dignity and admiration. They are a good dad to their kids, always listening, leading and lauding them. Family time trumps any other time spent away from loved ones. A Marrying Man leads his wife and children spiritually, relationally and financially. He is on top of things in his family and will never abdicate his role to another. He allows God's Word to shape him into His original plan and purpose for his life.

Wedding Women

The marital role of the wife is clear,

> *"Wives, submit to your own husbands, as to the Lord."* [15]

The word *"submit"* is not a popular word in our western culture, especially when it comes to relationship and even marriage. But let's look at the biblical meaning of this word. According to the Strong's dictionary of Bible words this word was a Greek military term meaning *"to arrange [troop divisions] in a military fashion under the command of a leader"*. In non-military use, it was *"a voluntary attitude of giving in, cooperating, assuming responsibility, and carrying a burden"*.[16]

A Wedded Woman nurtures, loves and supports her husband.

Biblical submission is voluntary. Just like the church submits to the headship of Christ voluntarily, the wife submits freely to the headship of her husband. Together they form an army; a spiritual force to annihilate the forces of evil around them. Good military commanders lead from the front and good soldiers do not break rank until the battle is won. The primary role of the husband is to love his wife. That does not mean that the

15 Ephesians 5:22 NKJV
16 Strong's Concordance Greek #5293. (Emphasis added)

wife cannot or should not love her husband. She could and she should. Love needs to be answered with love. Submission works in similar fashion. When you assume the role the Lord assigned to you in marriage and submit your life to God and to your own husband, then you allow your man to step into his assigned role and be submitted to Christ. We read,

> *"Submit to one another out of reverence for Christ."* [17]

The fear of God in a marriage keeps husbands and wives within the boundaries of their divine roles and functions.

A Wedded Woman nurtures, loves and supports her husband. She mimics what believers do with God. She stands by her man and salutes him with pride and passion. She follows him as he follows Christ. She completes him, makes him look good and carries him with encouragement, prayer and emotional support. As a carrier she nurtures their dreams and protects their vision. She passionately establishes an environment where her husband can share his dreams and secure his fears. She's dependable and understanding and is his best cheerleader.

> **The strength of a woman is not measured in muscle power. It is not displayed on the surface of her body, but deep in her heart.**

Her influence in the marriage is amazing because of her submissive stance. She is able to sway a wayward husband through her actions, without uttering one word.[18]

The Virtuous Woman

The Bible depicts women as strong and virtuous, not weak or inferior to men as many would want you to think.

---

17 Ephesians 5:21 NIV

18 1 Peter 3:1 NKJV *"Wives, likewise, be submissive to your own husbands, that even if some do not obey the word, they, without a word, may be won by the conduct of their wives."*

> *"Who can find a virtuous woman? For her price [is] far above rubies."* [19]

The Hebrew word for *"virtuous"* here means *"strength, might, efficiency, wealth, ability."* [20] According to Gesenius's Lexicon it means *"strength, power and might (especially warlike), valor."* It also means *"virtue, uprightness, integrity and even fitness"* A virtuous women is a strong woman, someone who will not surrender to evil, knowing that God has forged in her spirit a strength that can only come from Him. She was woven together in her mother's womb with the fabric of God's fortitude so she would be able to carry the blessings, vision and purposes of her husband and family. She excels in all forms of excellence. She nurtures a victorious, winner's spirit instead of succumbing to a victim mentality. Her worth is not determined on earth, but was set in heaven! A virtuous woman's worth is far above rubies. The wealth of a man is not measured in his wallet, but in his wife!

The role of the virtuous woman is amazingly modern. The following verses depict a woman of strength within the demands of a busy day. They speak to all women through ages past and present, whether you are a full-time homemaker or a career woman. Let's look at the things that make a woman virtuous:

She is trustworthy.

> *"Her husband can trust her, and she will greatly enrich his life."* [21]

She's got his back, stands by his side and cheers him on. She is his greatest asset and not a liability.

---

19 Proverbs 31:10 KJV
20 Strong's Concordance Hebrew #2428
21 Proverbs 31:11 NLT

She is good and not bad.

> *"She brings him good, not harm, all the days of her life."* [22]

Society may want you to think that bad girls have all the fun. That is a wicked fabrication out of the pit of hell. Bad is overrated and good underestimated. The virtuous woman adds value to her man and never breaks him down in private or public. She is a bringer of good and not bad. She adds excellence, pleasantness, value, happiness and benefit because that is what the Hebrew word here means.[23] The word for harm here is also translated "evil" and means "malignant, bad, hurtful, and unhappy".[24]

The virtuous woman is truly extraordinary. She has such depth that no one can call her shallow.

She is hard working.

> *"She seeks wool and flax, and willingly works with her hands."* [25]

She is quick to roll up her sleeves for the sake of her family. She'll do anything to make it succeed, not only when backed into a corner or out of desperation. Her willingness characterizes her endeavors.

> *"She is like the merchant ships. She brings her food from afar."* [26]

Her bread is found in heaven and like a ship that carries exotic and essential foods not found locally, she searches the shores

22 Proverbs 31:12 NLT
23 Strong's Concordance Hebrew #2896
24 Strong's Concordance Hebrew #7451
25 Proverbs 31:13 NKJV
26 Proverbs 31:14 NKJV

of heaven in the Word of God to carry seeds of promise and hope, fruits of the Holy Spirit and the bread of life to her family. What she has to offer is not local or ordinary. Her qualities have been shaped, prepared and packaged from afar, loaded into her spirit by the Master Himself.

She plans her days and serves her household with love and devotion.

> *"She gets up before dawn to prepare breakfast for her household and plan the day's work for her servant girls."* [27]

I have found that Sharon loves to plan her days. She does not need a minute by minute layout, only a sense of knowing where her schedule is taking her and with what activities she'll be busy with. This eliminates frustration and stress that can arise otherwise. Although she is not an early morning person, she is willing to get going at any time when our schedule responsibility demands it.

She is industrious and visionary.

> *"She goes to inspect a field and buys it; with her earnings she plants a vineyard."* [28]

She identifies uncultivated areas, acquires them with price and sacrifice and then invests in these areas by sowing precious seed in them. These unproductive fields in her household's lives soon become fruitful vineyards with abundant harvests. Somehow a woman has a wonderful ability to recognize and identify uncultivated areas in her husband's life. She finds ways to transform these areas into productive places within him.

---

27 Proverbs 31:15 NLT
28 Proverbs 31:16 NLT

She infuses enthusiasm and strength.

> *"She is energetic and strong, a hard worker."* [29]

The strength of a woman is not measured in muscle power. It is not displayed on the surface of her body, but deep in her heart.

Her exploits are profitable and she provides light for her loved ones.

> *"She makes sure her dealings are profitable; her lamp burns late into the night."* [30]

A mother is a night light for her children and a beacon of hope for her husband.

She is not idle.

> *"Her hands are busy spinning thread, her fingers twisting fiber. She watches over the ways of her household, and does not eat the bread of idleness."* [31]

She has a sense of inner soul-direction. Her moral compass points north and she has an uncanny ability to guard and watch over the life-direction of her family.

She is charitable and compassionate.

> *"She opens her arms to the poor and extends her hands to the needy."* [32]

---

29 Proverbs 31:17 NLT
30 Proverbs 31:18 NLT
31 Proverbs 31:19, 27 NLT
32 Proverbs 31:20 NIV

As a true nurturer and gatherer, she identifies needs and will do her utmost to meet the needs of those around her. It is a fact that women often times are stirred into compassionate action before men are.

She provides warmth to her family.

> *"She has no fear of winter for her household, for everyone has warm clothes."* [33]

Instead of bemoaning the terrible atmospheric conditions she and her family may face, she finds ways to bring warmth and comfort amidst such adverse conditions and circumstances.

She brings comfort to her household and takes care of her appearance.

> *"She makes tapestry for herself; her clothing is fine linen and purple."* [34]

She is the beauty in her husband's life and maintains her appearance for him like that of a blossoming rose in full sunlight on a summer's day.

Marriage works because you work at it

Her creativity and industry is in high demand.

> *"She makes fine linen garments and sells them, and supplies sashes for the merchants."* [35]

She is wanted and needed because of what comes from her life and actions. She gives much more than just a piece of her mind, she shares her heart.

---

33 Proverbs 31:21 NLT
34 Proverbs 31:22 NKJV
35 Proverbs 31:23 NKJV

She is defined by her inner strength and not her outerwear.

> *"She is clothed with strength and dignity; she can laugh at the days to come."* [36]

She is fully prepared for whatever may lay ahead. Although she does not know the future, she knows the One who holds the future. When she looks ahead it is not with dread and a sense of hopelessness, but she laughs at tomorrow because it is secure in the hands of her Creator and because she knows that it contains many unearthed blessings yet to be discovered.

She shares her wisdom and mentors with kindness.

> *"When she speaks, her words are wise, and she gives instructions with kindness."* [37]

Be a dream-realizer to your spouse

Life is so precious it simply must be shared. Instead of isolating herself from it, she immerses herself in it. She lives it to the fullest and shows others the beauty of it.

She is acknowledged and appreciated.

> *"Her children stand and bless her. Her husband praises her. Charm is deceitful and beauty is passing, but a woman who fears the Lord, she shall be praised. Reward her for all she has done. Let her deeds publicly declare her praise."* [38]

The virtuous woman is truly extraordinary. She has such depth that no one can call her shallow. She is not someone who, after reading Proverbs 31, made a checklist of these "good

---

36 Proverbs 31:25 NKJV
37 Proverbs 31:26 NLT
38 Proverbs 31:28,30,31 NLT

things" and now tries to conquer these challenges set before her. No, these qualities rise from her spirit as she surrenders to the Lord and devotes her life to Him and to her husband. These are not merely things she does, but it is who she is.

A Crown not a Trophy

You are not a trophy wife. Scripturally you are a crown wife. A trophy wife is someone who is sculpted on the outside. Typically with an older man, a trophy wife exists as a bragging right for the man. Her outer form reminds him of his youthful, lost strength. She is nothing more than an object to him. A crown wife is so much more! According to Proverbs 12:4,

"A virtuous woman is a crown to her husband"

A trophy is displayed but a crown is worn. A trophy speaks of a past victory while a crown speaks of a present authority. A trophy is empty and most often made of inferior material but a crown is filled with precious stones like diamonds, rubies, emeralds and other treasures. A trophy has symbolic value but a crown has real value.

As the crown of your husband you represent him. Your life is not about yourself. You are not a mere outer shell. Your value is measured spiritually by what God placed in you first and that value permeates through your whole being. You can make your husband proud. You add value to his life. You are not a mere decoration or after thought. You are the crown that demonstrates His authority and influence. As a virtuous woman you have an obligation to yourself. Look after yourself. Do not let the gold lose its luster. Do not let the diamonds of your life become dull and dim. Don't lose that sparkle in your eyes and the radiance on your countenance. If necessary, whip your body into shape. After all it belongs to your spouse.[39]

---

39 1 Corinthians 7:4 *"The wife does not have authority over her own body, but the husband does. And likewise, the husband does not have authority over his own body, but the wife does."*

Take good care of what belongs to him. Make yourself presentable to him. Use the make-up you need, spend time on yourself. Represent him to the best of your ability and you'll not only bless him but you too will be a beneficiary through the process.

Marital Dangers and Pitfalls

Marriage is under a brutal attack from the enemy. He will stop at nothing to see that marriage as a sacred institution be abolished, perverted and abused. He knows that marriage the way God intended is a potent weapon that liberates individuals to reach their full and divine potential in life, while establishing a pure and perfect environment for children to grow up in the best way possible. Marriage is a mirror image of what the strongest possible relationship in heaven looks like. It reminds him of our future fellowship and perfect companionship with Almighty God.

We need to be vigilant to strengthen our marriages and be quick to identify the obstacles and pitfalls that the enemy puts in our way. We simply cannot allow his evil tactics to invade our band of holy matrimony.

Role Reversals

Once we know our role and function in marriage we should never step into our spouse's role. We must stay in our lane. Too many times husbands abdicate their function of coverer and start carrying, or wives try to fulfill their husband's role to cover their family. In many marriages there are men not stepping up and women who are overstepping. Remember, when you are occupying your spouse's place in your marriage you are stopping them from being what the Lord called them to be. As long as you are playing their part, they will be forced to be something different. Be sure to fulfill your divine role. Simply be who the Lord has made you to be within your marriage and your spouse will be able to step into his or her function with much greater ease. It must be said that in today's modern age practical marital roles may not fit more traditional times. Some husbands work from home while their wives are employed in the corporate world. While practical roles can be shaped to fit the family demands, the spiritual roles of husbands and wives stay unchanged.

Excuses and Expectations

People love to hide behind excuses. "The reason we are getting a divorce is that we fell out of love." The fact is that love is not a feeling; it is an act of your will. Marriage and life for that matter does not work outside of the principles of the Word of God. You cannot seek the blessing of it without applying the principles that come with it. If you apply for a job because of the great benefits and paycheck each month, but do not show up to work on a daily basis to comply with the stipulations of your employer, do not think for one minute that you'll still qualify for the benefits and paycheck. You'll lose your job and those precious benefits.

Making Marriage Work

Marriage works because you work at it. It is one thing to establish a marriage, but you have to continue to strengthen your marriage, maintain what you've gained and even revive some areas that have been neglected. Marriage works because you work at it. If only couples put as much planning and work into their actual marriage as they do in the marriage ceremony itself! Hours of work go into the dress, the cake, the invitations, the seating arrangements, the legalities and honeymoon. No wonder it is such a special day. No wonder we have such fond memories of that glorious day. Come on, put some planning into your marriage. It is a life-long commitment and not a day-long ceremony! Find special ways to bless your spouse. Stir up your love for each other again. Do things together again. Write silly, romantic, and even naughty

Marriage is a life-long commitment and not a day-long ceremony!

notes to each other again. Shoot a love e-mail at your spouse. Stop waiting for your marriage to make you happy, you make it happy!

One day while we were pastors at The Cross Community Church in Ohio, my schedule was particularly busy. I noticed that my secretary made an appointment with a Mrs. Smith for two hours. I had no idea that Sharon called the church office and made that appointment. For that day, she was going to be Mrs. Smith and she had her man all to herself for two hours! Needless to say both of us were blessed by Sharon's ingenuity.

Cultivate mutual respect for each other and find ways to push each other forward. Be a dream-realizer to your spouse. Avoid things that annoy your better half. Go out of your way to bless him or her. Never, under any circumstances, criticize or speak negative about your spouse to others. Your sharp words will poke holes in your covering or carrier. If your covering is full of holes he will no longer be able to provide a protective shield for you to flourish in. When the challenges of life, like a thunderstorm, beats down on you and if your sharp words have punctured your covering you are going to get wet. If you poke holes in your carrier, she'll leak all your dreams, desires and blessings.

Marriage is about making memories together.

If, after an argument, you run to your parents and tell them how bad your spouse is, you cause them to pick up your offense. Now they are mad at your spouse and you feel good because they sided with you. Let's say you sort things out with your spouse, love spills over your disagreement and you are once again the two love birds, cooing the same beautiful romantic tune together, and your parents still have a bone to pick with your spouse. They were not part of the make up process and their negative attitude now muddies their relationship with your spouse and you have a hard time wondering why. Breaking down your spouse to make you feel better about yourself speaks volumes about your own insecurity. It is time to work out your own insecurities instead of projecting them onto your spouse. Putting someone down in order to lift you up is nothing short of destructive behavior. A principle that is ingrained into life itself is the principle of reciprocity: do unto others what you want them to do to you. The Bible says,

> *"With the same measure you measure it shall be measured unto you."* [40]

Measure out blessings towards your spouse and about your spouse to others and those blessings will be multiplied and returned back to you.

Marriage is about making memories together. Unfortunately too many couples spend too much time making negative memories. Do things that will produce, stimulate and imprint positive memories into the heart of your spouse so that when you two think of each other any bad memories are completely overwhelmed by the awesome times you have together. Do not wait for a funeral one day to voice what a good person your spouse was. Tell them today; better yet, show them. Laugh often and enjoy the funny moments of life. Instead of laughing at, laugh with them. Be determined to identify the beauty of life in each other. Instead of focusing on the flaw within your diamond, rejoice at the sparkle of it. All diamonds have flaws but are still valuable. Even a rough, uncut diamond is preferred over a polished piece of glass!

---

40 Matthew 7:2

Prayer Application

Dear Heavenly Father
May the vows I declared before You and my spouse remain sacred to us. Weave the two of us together so that we will be one. Give me strength to be who You made me to be and to step into all You have destined for us in marriage. Help me to identify the dangers and pitfalls for our marriage and give me agility and ability to avoid them.
In Jesus name.
Amen.

Notes:

Chapter 7: Intimacy

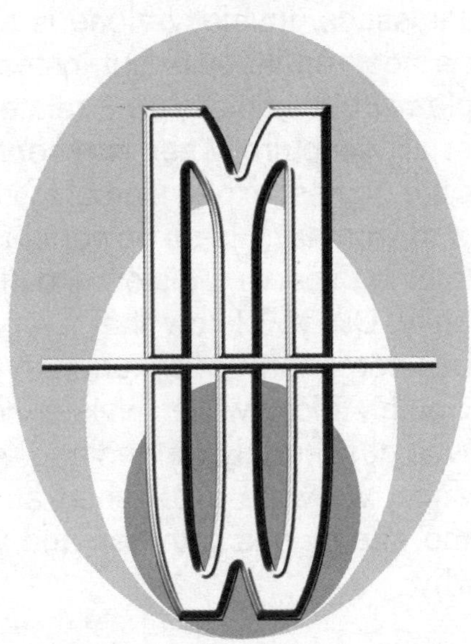

Macarena Men And Waltzing Women

It takes two to tango, a dance that is filled with rhythm, passion, timing, and movement. It is well known that men and women have unique rhythms of their own. In life men are like the Macarena and women are like the waltz. The Macarena is a feel good, make-me-happy dance. The waltz is a very romantic, slow-paced, and more complex dance. The two cannot be further apart. In marriage husbands and wives however take on the tango together.

A book like this would be incomplete without dealing with intimacy and sexual issues. Intimacy alone is a large enough issue to warrant a book on its own, but instead we'll look at some key principles about intimacy as it relates to the scope of this book. After all, scripturally sex is reserved exclusively for marriage. It is the highest expression of intimacy and unity between a man and woman. It is so powerful that the enemy has stopped at nothing to pervert, distort and plunder the sexual side of humanity. Did you know that every satanic ritual has some form of sexual perversion in it? In South Africa, while ministering to Satanists who desperately wanted and needed deliverance, we were astonished at the obsession the enemy has with sex and we discovered why.

Sex is God's invention. He made it for us to enjoy

Sex is God's invention. He made it for us to enjoy. He is not against it! He made us sexual beings. Unfortunately sex has been a taboo subject for so long among believers. We have allowed the world to shape acceptable boundaries for sex in our culture and the church has responded with emphasis on why this worldly kind of sex is wrong. It leaves people with the impression that God is against all forms of sexual activity and that a truly holy life has to be sexless. Let's set the record straight.

Inspirational intimacy

God gave sex to a husband and wife to enjoy and as a powerful bonding agent of unity. Sex in marriage is so potent that the enemy is terrified of it because it unifies more than flesh but spirit too. Sexual intercourse seals the eternal covenant between husband and wife. It is the activation of a key verse in the Bible,

"Therefore a man shall leave his father and

mother and be joined to his wife, and they shall become one flesh." [1]

This verse is so central to God's message to humanity it is also quoted by Jesus and the Apostle Paul. Jesus, when asked about the validity and acceptability of divorce, said,

> *"Have you not read that He who made [them] at the beginning 'made them male and female,' and said, 'For this reason a man shall leave his father and mother and be joined to his wife, and the two shall become one flesh?' So then, they are no longer two but one flesh. Therefore what God has joined together, let not man separate."* [2]

Jesus used the term *"one flesh"* to describe the unity between husband and wife. In marriage true unity is established. This oneness is forged on three levels, namely spiritually, emotionally and physically. To better understand the significance of this unity we should think of the concept of the Trinity. Scripture refers to the Father, Son and Holy Spirit. They are not three Gods, but One. The three Persons of the Godhead are distinct in function but one in action. This unity displayed in the Godhead is on many levels a mystery to humanity, but in serving God we explore and discover the love of the Father, the grace of our Lord Jesus Christ and the fellowship of the Holy Spirit.[3] When God says the husband will be joined to his wife and they will be *"one flesh"*, we should see it in similar light. How can two persons become one? We have already pointed out the differences between husbands and wives in this book. How then do we explain *"one flesh"*? God's concept of unity is amazing! In fact there is no greater weapon than what He describes as unity. Jesus said,

---

1 Genesis 2:24 NKJV
2 Matthew 19:4-6 NKJV
3 2 Corinthians 13:14

> *"If two on earth agree (harmonize together, make a symphony together) about whatever they may ask, it will come to pass and be done for them by My Father in heaven."* [4]

God sees sexual intercourse as much more than just "getting together" or as mere feel good physical contact. When there is a connection between two computers, a variety of things can be exchanged between them like e-mail, photos, documents, data and even system settings can be changed on both machines. Similarly during sexual intercourse there is an exchange on a natural and spiritual level. Naturally DNA is shared and spiritually soul-ties are established with your partner. In fact, you are sharing your soul essence with a significant other, giving them access to all of you. You are "one" with your spouse from that moment on. In marriage, husband and wife form a significant symphonious partnership that enables them to stand the test of time, defend the principles of godly life and penetrate divine destiny together. They form such a strong bond that nothing will be impossible to achieve and no blessing will be beyond their reach. Every time a husband and wife get together in sexual intercourse this bond is strengthened and they can truly enjoy the pleasures and beauty of this intimate act.

Spice up and sizzle

Let's face it, sex feels great and is wonderful. Take time for intimacy. Explore each other's bodies, wants and desires. Do it within the boundaries of purity. Take pleasure in each other with dignity. Sex should always be an adventure, a venture of togetherness. Let the journey be to strengthen the bond between you. Part of what makes sex feel good is the sharing of the moment of heightened pleasure. Enjoy it often. When you spend more time quarrelling with than pleasuring each other, your marriage is not going to be a happy one. Explore each other. Your spouse is an unending treasure map that will

---

4 Matthew 18:20 AMP

lead you to unearth amazing discoveries of bliss. Remember it is always better to give than to receive. Giving of yourself ensures a getting from your spouse. Sex is not primarily to be satisfied by your spouse. It is about satisfying your spouse. When you approach it with such an attitude you will both benefit in gratifying ways.

We have heard people speak of "makeup" sex too often. They use intimacy to mend fraying fibers of their marriage. It certainly has its place, but it is sad to think that the only times of intimacy they get is after a hurtful argument. There is something better than "makeup" sex. It is to "wake up" sex. Stir up your desire for each other. Spice up your relationship. Within the borders and boundaries of a godly lifestyle, sex is the most beautiful expression of God's desire for a husband and wife to celebrate the unity and bliss found in each other.

Change things up. Do not get stuck in a sexual rut. Do not allow monotony to suffocate your adventures in intimacy. Seize the moment and ignore time restraints. Schedule your private rendezvous if you think your life is too busy. Make an appointment for it and make preparations to make it unforgettable. There are moments for quick fixes and times for lingering pleasures. Allow yourselves both. Such moments are what should create memories in a marriage, snapshots of happiness that become the premise and conclusion of the adventure novel the two of you create together. There are chapters of joy and intrigue that needs to be completed that only the two of you can write together. For example: Chapter one, "It started one rainy night, a jazz tune playing on the radio. The air was filled with her sweet perfume and as I gazed into the laundry room, there she stood. . ."

Sex can never be a one night stand. It reaches into eternity and releases potency in the lives of a married couple

Romance does not start on the page of a novel or on a movie

screen. It is up to you to seize an everyday moment and fill in the pages of your story together with love, intrigue, seduction and desire. Set the pages of your love story on fire.

Reserved for Marriage: The Soul-tie of Sex

Satan's main objective is to bring separation between God and man. His aim is to separate and cut creation off from the Creator and sex is one of the weapons he uses to accomplish this. Marriage is God's prime example of the opposite of Satan's plans. God joins together! Sexual intercourse is the act where husband and wife join together, but this joining exceeds the realm of the physical. God is involved here. Sex between unmarried couples is a perversion at best. Think about it. Soul ties with a spouse are greatly desirable because these ties establish a bond of unity. But every time you have sexual contact with someone you tie your soul to that person. With promiscuity and adultery so rife in today's culture people are so entangled in a web they cannot escape from. They are all soul-tied up, connected to people in ways they never should be. What was designed to be beautiful becomes repulsive. The marriage-glue made to unite becomes a sticky mess that traps you in emotional and spiritual turmoil of regret. What is holy becomes sinful and what was destined to bring peace and harmony now leaves discord and guilt instead. Sex is never just physical.

Intimacy establishes a marriage. It is the physical activator of a marriage.

Sex can also never be a one night stand. It reaches into eternity and releases potency in the lives of a married couple that serves as an unbreakable bond that reflect the glory of God in unity. The strength of marriage is exponentially increased through intimacy. Sex between husband and wife is pure. It is a holy act of unity, connecting two people on a deep spiritual level. Sex is an act of creation, not just in procreation but every time sexual intercourse is enjoyed a stronger bond between husband and wife is formed. Why not use it as a holy weapon from the arsenal of heaven, and wield it together, as God intended within the framework of holy matrimony? With it you'll reinforce a godly unity between you and your spouse. It keeps your connection to each other exclusive, holy and special.

Procreation

Sex is also God's way to multiply His masterpiece of humanity. His command to Adam and later to Noah was to,

> *"Be fruitful and multiply."* [5]

New life springs up from intimacy. What a wonderful idea. Without intimacy between a man and a woman humanity would become extinct. God's original and normal concept of procreation was intimacy between husband and wife. But it need not be a chore or be reserved only for seasons when babies are desired. Remember, marital sex is beautiful and pure. It should be enjoyed for what the Lord made it to be, to establish and affirm unity in marriage and to create new life.

Ideologies of Intimacy

Intimacy establishes a marriage. It is the physical activator of a marriage. It unites a husband and wife and makes them one flesh. When you look at the word "Intimacy" something remarkable jumps out at you, "In-to-me-You-see". It is truly about transparency and vulnerability. Being intimate with your spouse allows them to see deep into your being as you share yourself exclusively and unreservedly with them. Unity produces a strength that even the enemy of our souls cannot negate. It also revives a marriage. Often times a husband and wife drift apart because of the business of schedules or the circumstances of life. Intimacy is the rope that secures them to each other again. Neglected intimacy produces weak and sick marriages. Starving your spouse sexually simply to get your way is unscriptural. Did you know that your body does

---

5 Genesis 1:28, Genesis 9:1, Jeremiah 23:3

not belong to you? God's Word is clear,

> *"The wife does not have authority over her own body, but the husband does. And likewise the husband does not have authority over his own body, but the wife does."* [6]

God's intent for intimacy was never to use it as leverage on your spouse or as a method for manipulation to get what you want. Such uses pollute the purity of intimacy and warp the holy nature of it, even within marital context. Your attitude must not be just "taking by demand". Remember in marriage we are to *"submit one to another out of reverence for Christ."*[7] Therefore the act of sex is not one of demand but of giving.

Intimacy plays a big role in the revival of a marriage. It creates a spark to start the fire of love burning again. It is the combustion chamber that will activate forward movement in a marriage again. It is the deepest way to express your mutual love for each other.

There are several books on the market that are dedicated to the wonderful subject of intimacy. We recommend every husband and wife to spice up their intimacy.[8]

We want to close this chapter with some grooming and beautifying tips for couples:

Men

It is important to look good to your spouse. A clean body, trimmed hair and nails, sparkling teeth and a sweet smell go a long way to wow your spouse. Even if you are out of shape and think you have already landed your catch does not mean

---

6 1 Corinthians 7:4 NKJV

7 Ephesians 5:51 NIV

8 "Intimate Issues" by Linda Dillow and Lorraine Pintus;
The Language of Sex: Experiencing the Beauty of Sexual Intimacy in Marriage, Dr. Gary Smalley, Ted Cunningham

you should not bait your hook for her again! It will demonstrate your intent to be the best for her. Making her feel important is what it is all about. She will appreciate the attention and extra effort you make. If you want special treatment from your spouse then apply some special treatment on yourself first. Sweep your lover off her feet every so often. Treat her like that fairy-tale princess and she will see you as her prince charming. Add some planning to an otherwise normal day and even a little special treatment will go a long way.

Treat her like that fairy-tale princess and she will see you as her prince charming

Women

Wives, make your man look in your direction. Do your hair and nails, color your lips and mascara your eyes. Go to town for him, and make sure he knows it is all for him. If you feel invisible then make it impossible for him to ignore you. I was speaking at a Women's Conference in Ohio and was sharing on this same subject. Every so often women would complain that they play second fiddle to football or work or something else. I said, "A sure way for you to be noticed and not ignored is to dress in a red ribbon around your neck. Make sure it is big, red and beautiful because it will be all you will be wearing! Go stand before the TV and see what happens. You will no longer be invisible to him." There was a giddy excitement in the room. On Sunday Rudi and I were ministering in the church and while we were sitting on the front row waiting for the start of the meeting, several couples came up to me. A man said, "I do not know what you said to the ladies yesterday, but I want to thank you and please come back again!"

Another lady mentioned to me before she went home after the Women's Conference she stopped at the hardware store and bought some red paint. She painted one wall red in their bedroom and spruced things up a bit. She lit candles and created an atmosphere that shouted, "I love you, come love me!"

Your Romance Rendezvous

Create a place of escape for you and your lover. Your bedroom should be a kid free zone, the place where romance happens. It is not the place to hang the family portrait. Your intimate moments should not be intruded upon. Make your bedroom a personal retreat away from worries and cares and the business of life. It should be an oasis of love, romance and sensual desire and not of clutter, dirty laundry and old stale smells. Whip things into shape. Spruce up your love zone, and set the atmosphere for love. Fragrant candles, soft music and naughty notes can go a long way in setting the mood. Make your bedroom your favorite place to be.

Why should your marriage be dull and void of excitement? Stop treating your marriage as a living entity. You are the excitement in your marriage. You are the spunk it needs. You are the solution. Use the girly visual elements God has given you and use the lingerie props in your bedroom. Disclose Victoria's secret to your husband before Victoria does it herself. Let the twinkle in your eye say it all to your spouse, "Come here, you are mine!"

> **Stop treating your marriage as a living entity. You are the excitement in your marriage. You are the spunk it needs.**

But you should also realize that true cleanliness and sex appeal flows from deep within. My parents used to tell us, "Even if a monkey wears a golden ring he still stays an ugly thing!" True beauty and real ugly is rooted in your heart. Just like you groom your body for the blessing and benefit of your spouse, and create special moments for each other to enjoy, both husband and wife should find and share inner peace, God-confidence, gentleness, genuineness and love. Allow God to fill your heart with the fruit of His Spirit[9], forgiving attributes and

---

9 Galatians 5:22 *"But the Holy Spirit produces this kind of fruit in our lives: love, joy, peace, patience, kindness, goodness, faithfulness, gentleness, and self-control. There is no law against these things!"*

the oil of joy. Put on the garments of praise for a spirit of heaviness. What your heart is embellished with will shine through to the surface of your life.

Enjoy your spouse in every way possible. He or she is God's gift to you. Satisfy him or her and you will be satisfied. You married your spouse so enjoy all the blessings married life was designed for!

Prayer Application

Dear Heavenly Father
Thank You for creating and designing intimacy as a sacred bonding agent of unity between me and my spouse. Help us both to seize these precious moments and enjoy this wondrous gift to us. Teach us the "Song of Solomon" together. May this bond of unity grow stronger in You as we celebrate our union and enjoy your gift in each other.
In Jesus name.
Amen.

Notes:

Chapter 8: Influence

Men of Means
And
Women of Worth

Men of Means and Women of Worth are people of influence. They exude a confidence that others are drawn to. In this chapter we will look at influence, value and finances. Let's start with influence. Finding a definition for influence is not as easy as it might seem. Dictionaries have several descriptions of the meaning of this word. Some say it means indirect power and authority. According to the concept of influence it means "an emanation of a spiritual or moral force" or "the power or capacity of causing an effect in indirect or intangible ways."[1] It comes from the Latin words *in* and *fluere* which means to flow into.[2] Influence is not something you can switch on and off. It automatically grows on you while it reaches out to others through you. You are an influencer whether you want to be one or not. Your life flows into that of those around you. Your life has the potential to shape someone else. Influence is persuasive, shaping and impressive.

The Bible refers to influence as dignity and honor. According to Psalm 112:9 righteous folks have influence,

> *"They share freely and give generously to those in need. Their good deeds will be remembered forever. They will have influence and honor."*

Far too many people have become exclusively impressionable. They reduced their lives to be influenced by others. They're glad to follow and in their own minds they feel disqualified to lead. They are influencees instead of being influencers.

> *"This is how the LORD responds: "If you return to me, I will restore you so you can continue to serve me. If you speak good words rather than worthless ones, you will be my spokesman. You must influence them; do not let them influence you!"* [3]

Influence is a tremendous gift of God

Mountain Moving Men and Wave Walking Women are leaders. Their lives are persuasive, their decisions contagious and their actions influential. Their circle or sphere of influence is always expanding. They are a

1 Merriam-webster Dictionary
2 Ibid
3 Jeremiah 15:19 NLT

force to be reckoned with because they are spokespersons for God. One thesaurus coins the phrase *"lead to believe"* as a synonym for influence.[4] Mountain Moving Men and Wave Walking Women are effective in "leading others to believe." They are people of authority. Leading is not merely something they do, it is who they are. They have this presence about them that makes others want to listen.

During our first Sunday service as new pastors in Elyria, Ohio a young man attended the meeting with his mother. He did not really care to be there, but his mother pleaded with him to accompany her to church that morning. The hand of God was evident on his life and Sharon started to minister to him in the power of the Holy Spirit. The Lord showed her that he was an influencer. Unfortunately he was influencing the young people of his generation in a destructive way, but God wanted to turn his life around. He crumbled in the presence of the Lord and yielded his life completely to God that morning. It turned out that he was a drug dealer and gang leader who now decided to serve God with all his heart. That night he brought several of his fellow drug dealers and gang buddies to the meeting. Every one of them accepted Christ into their lives as the power of the Gospel of Christ set them free from sin and bondage. The next few months were simply glorious in our church. Several hundred people came to the Lord, many influenced by the transformations in these young men's lives. Their hunger for God was phenomenal, their passion tangible and their influence in a formerly unreached segment of society unparalleled. We believe that influence is a tremendous gift of God every believer has to embrace and develop to be an effective witness for Christ in their community.

What really impacted us about influence is when we looked at the antonyms of the word 'influence'. Here are a few antonyms[5] for influence: impotence, inferiority, weakness, and in-

---

4 Thesaurus.com - influence, as a verb.

5 A word opposite in meaning to another

capacity. Wow, someone of influence leads a fruitful life. A life that births blessing, nurtures strength and breeds confidence. Value determines influence. If someone identifies you to have something of value, something they would like in their own lives they would be influenced by your actions.

Men of Means add value to the Kingdom of God. Theirs is not a superficial, external worth. They are not gold-plated iron, shiny on the outside, but ordinary at their core. God poured into them character and class. He knows they can handle blessings with dignity and wisdom. They are kingdom minded and not self-centered. They carry themselves as problem solvers and not trouble makers. Men of Means are equipped with the necessities to meet spiritual, emotional, relational and physical needs. They share their wisdom instead of giving you a piece of their minds; they reinforce godly principles instead of focusing on legalistic rules. If they come across a hungry man, they'll not only give him a fish, but also a rod, reel, hook and bait and teach him how to fish so that when hunger knocks on his door again he'll know how to generate food in his life. Men of Means have gumption. Their wealth cannot be measured on the stock market. It is not stored in bank vaults or under mattresses. They carry it inside their spirit and share it with those around them. They allow God to use them in such ways that people feel blessed and refreshed, equipped and encouraged. Men of Means are able men and their influence impacts the lives of those around them.

Women of Wealth also walk in the abundance of the kingdom of God, being confident in God's provision and satisfied with His measure poured into their lives. Their place in life is established and celebrated, They have true substance and not just empty shells. They use God's blessings to help others. They have a "can do" attitude to life. They know that,

> *". . . With God nothing is impossible."* [6]

---

6 Luke 1:37

And

> *". . . If God is for them, who can be against them?"*[7]

They exude God confidence above self confidence. Women of Wealth are also Women of Worth, valuing God first and foremost in their lives. Their worth is not defined by their pocket book or proficiency in life. Their worth is established by God in heaven. They are His treasures and that makes them tremendously valuable and marvelously positioned to bless those around them.

Together Men of Means and Women of Wealth can make a huge difference in the lives of many people. They share in the success of God's work in their lives and model the true nature of success and abundant living to the world. Their circle of influence continues to grow and they become a force to be reckoned with wherever they go.

They establish a new, scriptural definition of success that does not revolve around finances alone. We strongly believe that the Lord wants to bless us in every area of life and will cause us to excel in them all. Men of Means and Women of Wealth give God access to all these areas. They expose their strengths to be strengthened even more as well as their weaknesses, because the Bible declares,

Value determines influence.

> *"The weak can say 'I am strong'"*[8]

Finances

Money plays an important role in life. It is a tool with which we value things. We buy and sell with it. Money is a printed

7 Romans 8:31

8 Joel 3:10 NKJV

medium that determines monetary value. Without it we suffer. Having a wrong attitude about it will make us suffer. In South Africa we heard a saying: "When money leaves a household, love usually follows in its footsteps." It should not be so, but often times we found that money issues are at the root of most marital disputes.

Jesus, in speaking about your relationship with money said,

> *"No man can serve two masters: for either he will hate the one and love the other; or else he will hold to the one, and despise the other. You cannot serve God and mammon."* [9]

Mammon is wealth personified. In other words, when your life revolves around money (wealth, riches, and treasures) instead of your spouse you are serving mammon. When you allow finances to be a living entity in your marriage, it becomes the third party with whom you have a love affair. Are you are serving mammon? Are you cheating on your spouse with your money? Your mammon does not need to be big. You do not need a lot of money to serve mammon. In fact, it is very easy to personify money in the absence of it in your life. You idealize what you do not have, so serving mammon is not only something rich people should be concerned about.

Where God leads, He feeds and where He guides, He provides

Who is your Source?

God called us to *"be servants of Christ and stewards of the mysteries of God."*[10] We are to serve the Lord and manage all His blessings in our lives. In marriage we simply must identify our Source. Where God leads, He feeds and where He guides, He provides. Money can never be our source. Money is simply one of many tools through which God can bless us.

9 Matthew 6:24 NKJV
10 1 Corinthians 4:1

Sharon and I can echo the Apostle Paul's words,

> *"I know how to live on almost nothing or with everything. I have learned the secret of living in every situation, whether it is with a full stomach or empty, with plenty or little. I can do all things through Christ who gives me strength."* [11]

We learned how to thrive regardless of bank balances. Often people quote the second portion of this scripture and apply it to everything but finances, but the true context here is evident. Christ is our Source and Strength and with Him we can truly live regardless of the season we are in and He enables us to do all things.

I remember when we were planning to get married and we had to get all our ducks in a row for that wonderful day. I was a Bible School student and Sharon worked for a bank at the time. We met with Sharon's pastor for pre-marriage counseling and one of the suggestions he made was to draw up a marriage contract. He noted the legal protection such a document could bring in business matters. We went to see an attorney to comply. We wanted to do everything right and because we were so young we welcomed sound advice. During the interview with the attorney it soon became apparent that we were both starting from zero. We did not own much, but what we had we viewed as "ours" and not "mine". It was amusing to read that contract. Usually each spouse would list their assets at the time that would be excluded from the marriage. Everything they would acquire during the marriage would then be shared equally legally. On our contract there were no lists. We had nothing to list.

Throughout our married life God has been very good to us. We have lived in faith for our entire marriage. We received a

---

11 Philippians 4:12-13 NLT Emphasis Added

fixed, salaried assured income from an employer for only a fraction of our married life. There have been times of financial challenge and we've experienced times of wonderful blessing. We determined that our lives would not be defined by finances but by the Lord. Our value is not determined by our net worth.

One sure way to keep mammon out of your marriage is to name your every dollar. You heard me. Give it a name. Remember money does not have personality. It is simply a means to an end. Set up a budget and designate its purpose. Set it up together and live by it. Make your money work for you instead of you working for it. I remember when I proposed to Sharon and she excitedly accepted my proposal. We were getting married! It was a fantastic time in our lives. One day, while visiting with her, I asked to see her charge card. She was always very responsible with money, and had been saving for her future. She excelled in her work at a bank in South Africa and knew how to work with money. She did however use this charge card to purchase clothing on credit from time to time. She presented me with the card and I asked her for a pair of scissors. "I am marrying you and not your debt." I proclaimed. I continued to do plastic surgery on that card, as I reduced it to small plastic pieces. Right there and then we made an agreement with each other. We would not live with credit card debt. We would "pay as you go" and all financial decisions we would make together. If it was not in the budget we would formulate a plan of action together. This system has worked for us quite well over the years. Although I handle most of the day to day financial stuff, we are both on board and clued up on where we stand. A great resource for money matters is radio host and financial guru Dave Ramsey and we recommend his book, "The Total Money Makeover"[12] to transform your financial future together.

Budgeting

Making a family budget is really not difficult. Keep it simple.

---

12 See www.DaveRamsey.com

List your income on a paper. Account for every dollar. Then determine your tithe by dividing your total income by 10. (You can also multiply your income by 0.1 to determine your tithe.) Your tithe belongs to the Lord. It is your seed you sow back into the Kingdom soil. The Bible says,

> *"He gives seed for the sower and bread for eating."* [13]

I always say that generally you should not eat your seed or sow your bread. Your tithe is not an expense item. It is not something you pay. You simply return what does not belong to you anyway.[14] The tithe is also called your first fruits in scripture, so a good practice is to let your tithe be the first order of business every month. Put it on the top of your list and not the bottom. There are so many blessings attached to tithing that we cannot list them all here. The best way is to discover them for yourself as you tithe.

Next list your expenses. Start with the "needs" and end with the "wants". Typically you want to list your mortgage, utilities, etc. first. Things you cannot go without. This exercise is good to determine your financial priorities. A good practice is to save at least another tithe for retirement (depending on your current age). We encourage young couples to put something away every month for retirement. Compound interest is a wonderful thing especially over an extended period of time. You should also build up an emergency fund equal to a few months of income. When you have to replace a water heater, or fix an air conditioner or incur unexpected medical expenses, you can dip into this emergency fund. Each spouse should have a budgeted allowance to spend any

Financial success does not happen automatically. It requires prayer, planning, and perspiration

13 Isaiah 55:10 & 2 Corinthians 9:10

14 See the following verses on tithes, Leviticus 27:30, Deuteronomy 14:22, 2 Chronicles 31:5, Malachi 3:10, Matthew 23:23

which way they want. Dave Ramsey's envelope system[15] is a great practical way to budget in fact my dad introduced me to his own envelope system when I was still a young boy. The trick in budgeting is to name every dollar and stick to the budget. Any unbudgeted expenses should be discussed and approved by both you and your spouse. You'll learn to live within your means and be good stewards of what God gives you. Financial success does not happen automatically. It requires prayer, planning, and perspiration.

As parents, it is also your responsibility to teach your children responsible and sensible financial principles. I remember my first allowance. I was probably about 3 years old and my dad put money and an envelope in my hands. He said, "Here is your allowance for this month. Every month, I am going to bless you with some money and with it you can buy anything you like." I was so happy and immediately had visions of ice cream and candy bars bouncing around in my head. "What is this envelope dad?" I asked. He said, "This is a tithing envelope I picked up at church. I'll give you one with your allowance every month. Son, remember that 10% of your allowance belongs to God and you should place it in this envelope and give it to Him on Sunday at church." Of course dad had to tell me what 10% is and he also arranged with the church office to mail me a tithing receipt every month. For years it was the only mail I ever received, but I looked forward to receive it every month. It sent a message to me that my tithe was important to God and should never be taken lightly. Tithing has literally been part of our lives ever since. It is a non negotiable, prominent part of our financial success story.

Your true wealth is the influence God has given you

Dangers of Debt

Living beyond your means places your lives and marriage in a precarious situation. It is like stepping into a slow turning

15 See www.daveramsey.com

winepress that will squeeze the life out of you. As time passes pressure increases and adds terrible tensions into your marriage. Do not allow your wants to exceed your needs. Use sober judgment in allocating your finances. Let the Jones' keep up with themselves. Let them enjoy their expensive, bank financed automobile. Do not be embarrassed by your fully paid, trusty clunker. If they want to live their lives leveraged to the bank let them go ahead. Stuff your piggybank while they pay their debtors. Dave Ramsey always says, "Live like nobody else so you can live like nobody else." Image is short sighted, selfish and overrated but wisdom plans ahead, considers the cost and is totally underestimated.

Remember as Men of Means and Women of Worth you are not defined by what you own but by what you do. You are not measured in terms of dollars but of sense. You influence others because you were influenced by God, His word and His Spirit. You are positioned to successfully step into Divine destiny. Money works for you and not the other way around. Your value cannot be counted from a wallet or hidden in a bank vault and wealth is not heaped up but spread out. You live to be a maximized blessing to people around you. With an open heart, hardworking hands, feet stepping towards greatness you have turned your head toward wisdom.

As a Man of Means or a Woman of Wealth, your true wealth is the influence God has given you. Use it for His glory. You have the ability to shape lives and pour into them the love, goodness and grace of God. You can point them to where you are walking and encourage them to face God and not hide from Him. Influence is neither manipulative nor intimidating. Look at Jesus. He was a clear Leader, strong and decisive. He lived free from any outside interference of man, yet was powerfully connected to His Father in heaven. He was loving and caring, and gentle, sometimes in a forceful way. He was moved with compassion for people, faithful to His call and both inclusive and exclusive. Anyone had access to him, even little children, while at times He huddled together with His chosen twelve on a secluded mountain. He influenced others not by forced actions but unconditional love. He did it by practicing what He was preaching. He shared His worth and means with others. He was and still is the Giver of life. Let's follow His example by stepping into His footsteps. As Men of Means and Women of Wealth we are His hands extended here on earth.

Prayer Application

Dear Heavenly Father
Your Kingdom is not one of lack but abundance and I am not defined by what I own but by Whom I belong to. Thank You, Lord for being the God of more than enough. You are my Provider and You have gifted me. Let my focus be ever looking to You as my Source. May I never be distracted by the wealth and fame of others. Help me to be a good steward of what You have given me. Use me Lord, activate Your gifting and blessing in me to be flowing through me, touching others for Your glory. I will look to You.
In Jesus name.
Amen.

Notes:

Chapter 9: Conflict

Militant Men And Warrior Women

A man walked into a boardroom one day, having to face a notoriously difficult and combative group of men. His opening remarks were, "Men, I am not a fighter but I will not disappoint you." In this chapter we will look at warfare and conflict. We'll introduce you to spiritual warfare and discuss principles to properly deal with injustices and conflict. Mountain Moving Men and Wave Walking Women are not wimps or walkovers. They are not fighters, but they will not disappoint either. They stand for what is right and will fiercely defend the principles of truth, uphold the governance of justice and establish peace.

Mountain Moving Men are Militant Men and Wave Walking Women are Warrior Women. They realize the moment they became believers they stepped onto a spiritual battlefield. Jesus said,

> *"Blessed are the peacemakers for they shall be called sons of God."* [1]

Jesus used the term 'peacemaker' and not 'peacekeeper'. Peacekeepers are most often observers whose mere presence theoretically should maintain a measure of peace among warring factions. Peacemakers are not as passive. They are active enforcers of peace. They are soldiers in a spiritual battle between good and evil, light and darkness, heaven and hell. They observe and enforce, conquer and restore, fight and protect. Because this battle is spiritual in nature, their weapons are also spiritual weapons. The enemy is a spirit being. In fact, the primary battlefield for this war is in the minds of man. Satan is out to destroy humanity. He would love nothing less than to wipe you from the face of the earth. In opposing God, he opposes you too. You are the crown of God's creation. You are meant to step into a very exclusive place in heaven when your days on earth are completed; a place that once Satan himself occupied. Yes, he once served God in heaven. He was a prominent angelic being until He led a revolution in heaven and got expelled along with his cronies.[2] He is the enemy of your soul. He is your direct opposition. He is essentially behind the evil attacks on your life. He has set himself up to war against you and you must prepare yourself to both face and defeat him.

Peacemakers are not as passive. They are active enforcers of peace

1 Matthew 5:9 NKJV

2 Luke 10:17-20 / Isaiah 15 / Ezekiel 28

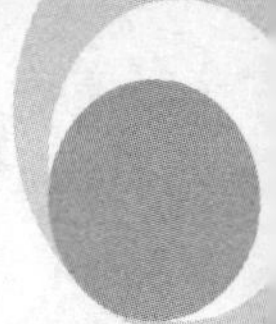

The Scripture says,

> *"For the weapons of our warfare are not carnal but mighty in God for pulling down strongholds"*[3]

You cannot fight a spiritual battle with physical weapons and you cannot use carnal methods to combat a spiritual foe. One of the great tactical ploys of Satan is to camouflage himself by hiding behind people, drawing your attention to them instead of exposing him as your true enemy. Militant Men and Warrior Women must first identify the true enemy. So often you rush into combat, wielding your words against a person you perceive to be opposing you, when the real threat is behind that person. Seek for the spiritual foe first. Identify the spirit of an attack and address that spirit in a scriptural way. Remember what God has given you.

> *"I have given you authority to trample on snakes and scorpions and over all the power of the enemy and nothing shall in any way harm you."*[4]

The amazing thing about being a believer is that you have the power to cast out demons, to expel them from infiltrating and influencing your life through circumstances. The beauty of this is that Jesus already conquered the enemy. Satan is a defeated foe trying to strike a final blow of desperation before he falls into the abyss of fire he is destined for.

Although his final move is a blow of desperation, it is nevertheless still potent and dangerous to the unsuspecting person. Scripture warns you to,

> *"Be sober and vigilant because your adversary the devil walks about like a roaring lion, seeking*

3 2 Corinthians 10:4 NKJV
4 Luke 10:18

whom he may devour." [5]

How to fight against temptation

Spiritual warfare is more about enforcement than conquering; about policing the principles of God in our lives. The enemy is identified as,

> *"A thief that only comes to steal, kill and destroy."* [6]

It is your duty to secure the backdoors and windows of your lives. You have to monitor and guard all the access ways and gates into your lives. You must watch what you look at, listen to and invest time in. Arrest the petty thieves before the flash mobs can mobilize. Nip illicit spiritual activity in the bud before it spirals out of control. If anger creeps in, let go and forgive while it is containable. If envy and jealousy rises up in you, focus on the grace and goodness of God in your life and rejoice in it and soon you will rejoice with the victory of others too. Temptations that wiggle their way into your mind must be pounced upon with boldness and without hesitation before they turn into sin in your heart. The Bible teaches to,

> *"Submit yourselves then to God. Resist the devil and he will flee from you."* [7]

The Lord gave me a tremendous revelation about temptations in our lives. I was reading through the book of Genesis and saw how the devil tempted Eve through a serpent.[8] My mind then went to Revelation 20:2,

> *"And he laid hold on the dragon, that old serpent, which is the Devil, and Satan, and bound*

---

5 1 Peter 5:8 NKJV
6 John 10:10
7 James 4:7 NKJV
8 Genesis 3:1

him for a thousand years."

In Genesis, during the opening chapters of God's history with humanity, the enemy is portrayed as a snake and in the closing chapters of Revelation that same enemy has become a dragon. Someone has been feeding the snake. It is one thing to kill a poisonous snake but to fight a dragon is a battle of epic proportions. We should kill the snakes of life before they can turn into dragons. Stop feeding your temptations with pitiful reasoning and selfish logic. Stop seeking excuses to wallow in weakness. Rise above the attack. Wield the sword of the Spirit, which is the Word of God. You are stronger than what the enemy wants you to believe!

Boredom is a breeding ground for temptations to grow strong in your life. Idleness is not a blessing. Stay busy. Fill your days with constructive things to do, even when you are in recreation or vacation mode. Temptations entice you to do something bad, but when you are already doing something good instead you will not be coerced that easily. The enemy will bombard your mind with destructive thoughts, but if you fill your mind with God's uplifting Word those worthless thoughts will have no place to attach themselves to in your life.

Choose your fights carefully. Only when you identify a viable enemy should you attack.

When to fight

You must determine what is worth fighting for. Stupendous amounts of your time can be spent on petty skirmishes designed to distract you from the real battlefield of your soul. Is it worth endangering your marriage because your spouse neglected to lower the toilet seat? Are you really going to waste your ammunition, intended for the enemy, on your better half because she cleaned and filed things in your study and now you cannot find them?

Choose your fights carefully. Only when you identify a viable enemy should you attack. Your spouse is not the enemy. Spiritual battles are much more important to win than physical arguments. One of the most successful ploys of the enemy is to hide behind the scenes. He'll do anything to get you to attack your spouse and unleash your wrath on the love of your life. Most of the casualties in marriage are a result of friendly fire. But when you recognize the intentions and ploys of the enemy coming against your marriage, you can unite with your spouse in a targeted attack against that real foe. Choose to be peacemakers and you'll be amazed at the glorious results. You will force the enemy to face you instead of hiding behind your loved ones.

> *"Two are better than one; because they have a good reward for their labor . . . though one may be overpowered by another, two can withstand him. And a threefold cord is not quickly broken."*[9]

One of the greatest benefits of marriage is the unity you share with your spouse. It is truly a mighty weapon that can accomplish just about anything. When you and your husband or wife stand together and enforce the principles of God over your lives and family, success is guaranteed, victory is ensured and abundance is secured. Each of you form a cord in your marriage and when you serve God together, He forms the third cord. There is no force that can break a marriage where these three cords have been entwined. Its tensile strength is incalculable.

There is no force that can break a marriage where these three cords have been entwined. Its tensile strength is incalculable.

Paul writes in Ephesians 6:12,

> *"We wrestle not against flesh and blood, but*

9 Ecclesiastes 4:9, 12 NKJV

> *against principalities, against powers, against the rulers of the darkness of this world, against spiritual wickedness in high places."*

When you see the enemy come against you, your spouse or loved ones, then you are obligated to rise up against him. In a wrestling match the object is to get your opponent off their feet and pin them to the ground. That is exactly what the enemy wants to do to you. Do not lose your footing. Position yourself with your spouse and gang up on the enemy. Show him that you will not settle for defeat, or accommodate his evil plans for your marriage and cringe with fear. Demonstrate your resolve in your calculated spiritual actions. Prayer will unsettle the enemy and knock him off his feet so you can pin him to the ground whenever he attempts to step into the ring with you. You can use the authority the Lord gave you by activating your faith. The Bible says,

> *"Submit yourselves to God. Resist the devil and he will flee from you."* [10]

Dealing with conflict

Every couple will face conflict. It is a natural part of life. Your character and moral fortitude is not demonstrated and celebrated during times of glorious marital bliss. They rise from the depths of your soul during times of challenge and conflict. During these times of difficulty you have the opportunity to showcase the true you God has been sculpting on the inside. Conflict arises when there is a difference of opinion that can easily be construed as personal rejection. It is your responsibility to learn to identify these moments of disagreements and to adjust towards your spouse's opinions and meet them half way. You would be wise not to perceive your spouse's outlook as a dismissal of your personal feelings, and lash out at them. It is so easy to say destructive things in a moment of anger, but so difficult to take those words back later. Quarrels appear

10 James 4:7

because of a variety of reasons. It could be a blatant demonic ploy to distract you and your spouse from the pathway to success and happiness. Or it could be because of the differences between husband and wife, man and woman. Conflict could also arise because of a past problem, present dilemma or a perceived fabrication. Sometimes a mere difference of opinion can trigger conflict situations. Conflict can even be stirred as a result of different parenting skills and models. Regardless of how and why conflict comes, husbands and wives need to learn how to deal with it in a Divine way. The Bible says,

> *"In your anger do not sin. Do not let the sun go down while you are still angry, and do not give the devil a foothold."* [11]

People are provoked to anger all the time. The Bible acknowledges that a person can get angry from time to time. In fact there is even a righteous anger that can stir a person to set wrongs right and take a firm stance for justice and righteousness. But the Bible warns us not to sin in our anger. Once aroused in anger, it is important how we channel that emotion. Do not waste that energy on sin. Sinning in your anger means to overstep God's permissions. Allowing foul language to pollute your mouth and cause a ringing in your spouse's ears, cursing them instead of blessing them, or raising your hand against the one you love. Another way to sin in your anger is digging up old sins that were forgiven and buried in the sea of forgetfulness.[12] Anger can even be misdirected. It may stem from a personal disappointment in your past and lashes out at others to mask its true origin. An unresolved emotional moment in your past is a perfect breeding ground for sinful anger. It attracts anger like a garbage dump attracts flies. Did you know that anger and rage is actually bad for you physically?

---

11 Ephesians 4:26-27 NIV

12 Micah 7:19 NIV "*You will again have compassion on us; you will tread our sins underfoot and hurl all our iniquities into the depths of the sea.*"

> *"I sat alone because of Your hand, for You have filled me with indignation. Why is my pain perpetual and my wound incurable, which refuses to be healed?"* [13]

Even righteous indignation, a positive kind of anger, can have negative results in your body. Anger literally can cause lingering and chronic pain.

Dr. John Sarno, a professor of clinical rehabilitative medicine in New York University School of Medicine, has treated thousands of patients with back pain. In the process of developing a diagnosis he began to question his patients with chronic back pain and discovered that 88% of them had a history of tension-induced reactions. Symptoms included: tension headaches, migraine headaches, eczema, colitis, ulcers, asthma, hay fever, frequent urination and irritable bowel syndrome.[14] Emotional pain can produce physical pain. It is important how you express your anger. If you do it in a way that is damaging to yourself and to others then it is sinful in nature. Another way not to deal with anger is to not express it at all. Repressed anger will also wreak havoc on your life. The Bible teaches us to,

> *"Be renewed in the spirit of your mind."* [15]

Condition yourself not to fight with your spouse but identify the spirit behind the conflict.

The spirit of your mind is your subconscious. It is in this region of your life where repressed emotion brews and if allowed, it influences and infiltrates the rest of your being. According to Dr. Colbert, anger is a conditioned response. You learn how to be angry when faced with

---

13 Jeremiah 15:17-18 NKJV Emphasis Added

14 Deadly Emotions by Dr. Don Colbert, MD, page 49 - 61

15 Ephesians 4:23 NKJV

a certain situation.[16] There are certain things that trigger your anger and you can re-teach yourself how to *"be angry and not sin."*

A second lesson we learn from Ephesians 4:26-27 is that we are to deal with anger in the present. We should not allow it to grow old or smolder overnight. *"Do not let the sun go down while you are angry!"* Deal with it immediately. Learn to apologize to others quickly. Confess your anger to God and receive His forgiveness right away. Another way to control your anger is to take a "time out." You can recollect your thoughts and refocus your mind. You can breathe deep and place your focus and thoughts on the Word of God while allowing the Holy Spirit to flood your soul. But remember the time out cannot last too long. It should merely be a breath catcher, a moment with God to re-direct your thoughts and emotions. Anger is rooted in pride. Learn to let go and let God have His way. Learn to not get so worked up about things people do, especially your spouse. Condition yourself not to fight with your spouse but identify the spirit behind the conflict. Join forces with your spouse and attack the enemy together. That way you will not allow the enemy to gain a foothold in your marriage.

I remember our first marital disagreement. It was in our first year of marriage and I could sense something was brewing in Sharon's mind for a day or two. I could not put my finger on it, but I knew I somehow messed up and did something that offended her. She initially gave me the silent treatment. I asked her. "Honey, what is wrong?" She looked at me intently and said, "You know what is wrong!" When I said I did not have the slightest idea, she shared her frustrations. Initially her complaints gushed forth like a fountain and I listened intently. After a while she got it all out of her system. I asked her if she was done. She

Let sleeping dogs lie, otherwise when awakened they will come back to bite you.

16 Deadly Emotions by Dr. Don Colbert, MD, page 49 - 61

nodded her head. Then I said, "Now here is my side of the matter." When I was done I said, "Now sweetheart, let's agree that in our marriage we are going to deal with conflict God's way." She wholeheartedly agreed and we prayed together right away. Forgiveness was both offered and received and the matter resolved. Ever since that day we have done our utmost to deal with any conflict by introducing God into the situation. Selfish emotions cannot stand a change when God steps in. How can you hold on to bitterness or unforgiveness when you deliberately invite the Lord into the conflict situation? Together we try to identify the real enemy and deal with that enemy in no uncertain terms.

Including others in your conflict: A Bad Idea

It is best not to include others into your personal differences with your spouse. When you respect each other, you will not include others in your arguments. Do not let anger cloud your judgment. Bringing others into your battles will complicate things considerably. Bringing your children into your conflict not only jeopardizes the bond of your family unit, but also teaches your children destructive behavior in conflict situations. Do not let them take sides or put them in such a position because they will despise you later. Do not discuss your spouse with your children in a derogatory manner. You are the parent, be one. There is a danger in sharing these things with your children. You place them in a position where they will feel pressure to comfort you. Adult stuff belongs in adult minds and hearts.

The same goes for your best friends. Speaking out against your spouse easily becomes a destructive habit and your friends will find ways to remind you just how bad your spouse is because you created such a negative view in their minds.

A better alternative is to pour your heart out to God, because He is the one who can do something about your situation, and when he forgives He forgets, unlike the ones you share your spouse's misdemeanors with. Keep your disputes personal and private. Set a good example for your children to follow. Teach them the importance of how to deal with and resolve conflict in a godly and timely manner. Lead by example. Your children will do what you do more than what you say.

Double Jeopardy

In South Africa we have an old saying, "Do not exhume the dead cow from the ditch." Its meaning is similar to "let bygones be bygones." During a heated argument, there is always the temptation to rehash your spouse's previous mistakes. You remind them of past faults and flaws in an effort to win a present disagreement. You pick at the bare bones like a dog guarding his favorite bone. There is no nutrition left. You get nothing good from it, other than making your spouse feel guilty all over again.

Think of a court judgment. When someone here in the USA is brought to justice, the prosecution has one chance to present their case. When the verdict is rendered and judgment is made, that individual cannot be tried for the same offense again. It is called the double jeopardy rule. How many times do you want your spouse to pay for what he or she did? Forgiveness should not have an expiration date. God's forgiveness does not and neither should yours. The Bible declares,

> *"For I will be merciful to their unrighteousness, and their sins and their lawless deeds I will remember no more."* [17]

When God forgives, He forgets. Let sleeping dogs lie, otherwise when awakened they will come back to bite you. Keep your disagreements in the present tense and deal with issues one at a time.

Stay away from Absolutes and Generalities

---

17 Hebrews 8:12 NKJV

People often talk in absolute terms. "You **always** pick your fathers side!" Or "you **never** pick up after yourself." Or even "you are late **all the time**." Using absolute terms like 'always' and 'never' can only escalate the conflict. Always and never is a long time! When you use these terms in frustration to give gravity to your argument, you also unwittingly introduce a lie into the conversation. If you say "you **never** bring me flowers", you had better be sure he never brought you flowers before. Build your conversations on truth and not lies. If you say "you're **always** against me watching football", then again make sure you are voicing the truth. Our experience is that when you use absolutes in a conflict situation they are seldom truths and often lies.

When you are in a specific conflict situation objectify the problem and not the person. Instead of saying "I hate **you** for not standing up for me", why not try "Honey, I felt isolated tonight and hope you will help me overcome this feeling. Can you pray with me for God to strengthen me and help me **overcome the feeling of isolation** in my life?" You have just identified the real issue and included your spouse to stand with you in dealing with it. You also communicated to your spouse how he or she can help you in the future.

Celebrate your spouse's strengths instead of attacking their weaknesses.

Football is more than a contact sport, it can also be a conflict sport. You have two teams with one focus: a leather ball. They seek to carry the ball and score a touchdown if possible or a field goal within their allotted time. Every once in a while the players get distracted. Their focus is turned from the ball to a player with nasty results. Fists are slung through the air and the game comes to a screeching halt. A team cannot win without the ball in hand. Fights and bad field behavior cannot be tolerated. Similarly in marital conflict you have to keep your eyes on the ball. Identify where your focus should be. Your spouse is for you and not against you. You should team up together and not break the ranks. Do not allow the enemy to stir things up between you and your spouse only for him to go and sit on the grandstand and watch the spectacle from a safe distance. Do not allow him to paint your spouse as the wide receiver of the opposing team that you have to tackle. Go together and pull the enemy from his passive seat, bring him into play and let him eat the dust he envisioned for you. Catch him with the ball and flatten him to the ground. Make him think twice before he attacks your marriage again. Instead of focusing on your spouse's blemishes why not take a moment for an attitude of gratitude towards him or her. Quickly find a positive to replace the negative. Celebrate your spouse's strengths instead of attacking their weaknesses. Instead of hashing out all the battles you face and describing the stature of the opponents in the opposition side, start calculating the blessings and past victories that you have won together. It is amazing how quick your combined morale can be boosted, not to mention the reality that God is your Coach and His team never loses. Find things you can be thankful for together. Remember, you are a team of two with God as your Coach, a threefold cord not easily broken. Play, fight and celebrate as a team.

When you are in a specific conflict situation objectify the problem and not the person

Discernment: Physical, Spiritual or Emotional?

You would do well to be in tune with your marriage partner's physical and emotional condition. If he or she is experiencing physical pain you can expect an emotionally compromised condition.

Women, your husband can come home fatigued and filled with work related stress. Know his demeanor and partner with him to alleviate these pressures that build up in him. Couples be sensitive to each other and do not allow these things to spill over into your home. Identify the stress your partner can be facing and instead of taking it personally help them work through it. Certain physical conditions can inflict emotional distress. Take responsibility and deal with it. Again, personify the condition as the enemy and not the person.

Men, during certain times of your wife's menstrual cycle she can experience PMS.[18] It is because of hormonal activity in her body. She might be irritable or a little depressed. Do not take it personally. It is hormones, not you. Ladies, we have found Pamprin works wonders. When you are sensitive towards your spouse's state of mind, you'll sidestep many potential conflict situations. Communication is so important. Voice your feelings, stresses, worries, joys and apprehensions with your spouse. Remember they cannot read your mind. Then pray for and encourage each other.

Men and women, sooner or later as they get on in years, face the dreaded change of life. Too many people buckle at the stress and challenges this season brings, and often results in otherwise stable and vibrant marriages to disintegrate. This need not be the case. Life is filled with constant change. Embrace it together.

Yes, there is an enemy out to get you. And yes, too often you fall for his devices and methods. But know that he is a defeated enemy, one that can only go as far as you will allow him in your life and marriage. Militant Men and Warrior Women know how to fight, when to fight and with whom to fight. They know that unity and intimacy are two of the most powerful weapons God gave them to nullify and neutralize the plans of the evil one in their lives. They are not fighters, but they surely will not disappoint, especially when it comes to spiritual warfare.

---

18 Pre Menstrual Stress

Prayer Application

Dear Heavenly Father
Help me to fight for what is right and not to waste energy on battles that don't matter. Secure the doors and windows of my life. Guard all the access ways and gates. Lead me not into temptation but deliver me from evil. Help me to fight against temptations. Strengthen our marriage so we can together take on the enemy and gain the victory. Remind me everyday that the enemy has been defeated and that I can walk in the victory You gave us.
In Jesus name.
Amen.

Notes:

Chapter 10: Identity

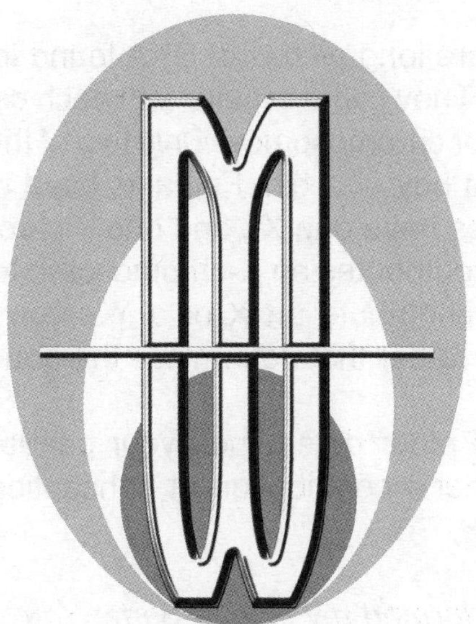

Manly Men And Womanly Women

You are God's handiwork and not a DNA disaster. He planned your life with precision and vision and gave you a hope and a future.[1] You are not required to fit into the molds of man. You are a God-original. If you want to be happy and successful in life you need to stay in the role God cast you in. He made humans male or female and that distinction

---

1 Jeremiah 29:11 NLT *"For I know the plans I have for you, says the Lord. 'They are plans for good and not for disaster, to give you a future and a hope."*

does not start and end with the differences in our physical bodies. Your gender starts in your blood, determined by your chromosomes.

Chromosomes are long pieces of DNA found in the center or nucleus of cells. They come in pairs with each cell in your body having 23 pairs of chromosomes. Only two of these determine if you are born a boy or a girl. Females have two X-chromosomes and males have one X-, and one Y-chromosome. The mother always contributes an X-chromosome to the child and the father may contribute an X or a Y chromosome. So in actuality it is the father that determines the gender of a child.[2]

Your Heavenly Father determined your gender even before your earthly father's contribution at conception. We read in Psalm 139:13-16,

> *"For You formed my inward parts; You covered me in my mother's womb. I will praise You, for I am fearfully [and] wonderfully made; Marvelous are Your works, And [that] my soul knows very well. My frame was not hidden from You, When I was made in secret, [And] skillfully wrought in the lowest parts of the earth. Your eyes saw my substance, being yet unformed. And in Your book they all were written, The days fashioned for me, When [as yet there were] none of them."*

God invested a lot of time on your identity. He made you unique and gave you an original set of finger prints, a unique pattern in your retina, distinct features that makes you, you. He knows who you are even when you sometimes do not. He does not make

You are God's handiwork and not a DNA disaster.

2 Healthscout.com - Reviewed By: David C. Dugdale III, MD, Professor of Medicine, Division of General Medicine, Department of Medicine, University of Washington School of Medicine.

mistakes or rejects. His is a work of perfection and you should embrace His handiwork in you.

Do not allow the enemy of your soul to shape your identity, nor anyone else for that matter. Refuse to fit into humanity's mold. You do not have to live your life like a square peg in a round hole. Celebrate who you are by knowing who God made you and live your life in that destiny.

Manly Men

If God made you a man, then be the man He made you to be. Unfortunately we've allowed secular society to shape the concept of manhood, casting a stereotype of what men should do and look like. Sometimes the pressures to fit into this mold can be immense. A boy that does not play football or excel in sports is oftentimes cast as an inferior, lesser man. His peers depict him as a womanly man or a sissy and a seed of misplaced identity is planted in his mind. Initially he would resist the notion that he is different, but oftentimes eventually would give into this erroneous depiction of himself. Peer pressure caused him to veer from God's tremendous plans with him as a Manly Man and he became a womanly man, resulting in an identity crisis often leading into homosexuality. An overpowering, controlling and smothering mother that takes charge in all arenas in her child's life can also form a twisted picture of gender identity. An absent dad and domineering mom can contribute to forming a false sense of identity in their child's life.

Another interference of man that opens a door to homosexuality is sexual abuse. This applies to both men and women alike. It is one of the most devastating things that can ever happen to a person. Being victimized sexually, especially at a young age, leaves scars on so many levels in a person's life. It violates trust and forces doors of emotional trauma to open and in many instances create a warped mentality to sexuality. It is so important for complete healing of such brokenness on every level. Every effort must be made to close those unnatural doors forced open through broken humanity. If ignored someone else's sin can become the abuse victim's iniquity.[3] Godly counseling is vital to the restoration process.

Something that is being touted in many schools as part of their sex education programs is to encourage youth to experiment with their sexuality, to discover for themselves what their sexual orientation really is, as if it is a simple choice on par with any other choices they would make in life. The truth is that you cannot choose your chromosomes. Remember that your Heavenly Father determined your gender. Homosexuality is not a genetic thing, it is a behavioral thing. You are not born with a concept of sexual identity. It is a learned behavior.[4]

Scripturally, homosexuality is sinful behavior.[5] The Biblical concept of sin is "to miss the mark." Sin causes all people to *"fall short of the glory of God"*[6] and has to be *"confessed and forgiven"*[7] to see God's plans and purposes restored in your life. In the Bible God clearly takes a stand against it. It is not because He hates sinners. In fact,

> *"God so loved the world that He gave His only begotten Son so that whosoever believes in Him should not perish but have everlasting life."*[8]

Homosexuality is in the same category as any other sin because all sinful behavior causes you to "miss the mark". To give in to sinful behavior is to turn you back on the loving

---

3 Iniquity comes from the root Hebrew word that means "to twist, distort, pervert or to bend".according to Strong's Concordance #H5753. (See Psalm 32:1-2, Psalm 5:1,5-7)

4 According to Dr. Richard Dobbins' article *Hope for the Homosexual* at www.drdobbins.com.

5 Genesis 19; Leviticus 18:22; Romans 1:26, 27; 1 Corinthians 6:6-10 (See also www.ag.org/top/beliefs/relations_11_homosexual.cfm).

6 Romans 3:23

7 1 John 1:9

8 John 3:16

Creator and His glorious purposes for your life. You will fail to realize your full potential and essentially settle to exist for a short while on earth in a form of life that resembles an empty shell. God's plans for you exceed the limits of carnality and stretches into eternity. You can joyfully embrace, enjoy and excel in both these realms of living. In the carnal world you experience physical existence here on earth and you were born into this realm.

God wants you to excel in it in every way, but remember that this life is merely a preparation for eternal life that follows. You get to know God here, develop your faith and devotion to Him here. He shapes you for what lies ahead. To miss the mark (target) here will affect your eternal outcome. If you reject God's purpose for you here, you will fail forever.

What does it mean to be a Manly Man? Simply put, a Manly Man embraces God's identity for his life. Although he shares many manly characteristics with other men, he also expects to find truly unique and identifying qualities that God placed in him from the beginning. He is man enough to resist being cast into one of society's molds. He is strong in his convictions, active in his faith and sensitive to the needs of others. Manly does not necessarily mean rough and tough.

God wants you to excel in it in every way, but remember that this life is merely a preparation for eternal life that follows.

Manliness is not determined by what you do but by who you are. You can be manly when hunting, cooking in the kitchen, fishing, decorating a room, playing music and playing football. You are not dependant on who others say you are. Do not allow your identity to be stolen or mistaken. Once you discover and realize who God made you to be then you are free to step into His role for your life. A confident man does not have to convince others of his manliness. When we look at the life of

David we find extraordinary characteristics that defined him as a man. He was a giant slayer, always strong in battle. He was an anointed musician. His leadership abilities were second to none as he trained up mighty men of valor. He wrote poetry in the Psalms, danced in worship before the Lord and even prayed that God would teach his hands to make war. He was a skilful hunter because he killed a lion and a bear and he was known as a MAN after God's own heart. This testimony of David's life is a great example for any man to model after.

Did you know that God anointed craftsmen to decorate the Tabernacle and the Temple?[9] These were not just architects, but also interior designers, who sewed and embroidered all the décor and embellishments according to God's direction. They were anointed by God to do so. They were manly men anointed to fulfill what God needed them for. A Manly Man is a gentleman. He is courteous and not rude, respectful and not critical, mild mannered and not evil tempered. In short, he is a man of God. Celebrate and enjoy your manhood.

Womanly Women

If He made you a woman, then embrace your womanhood with exuberance. Women are too often seen as the inferior gender. In God's eyes you are precious and special and equally impressive as your manly counterparts. Being a Womanly Woman has little to do with how you dress and what you do. It is who you are. God made you a woman and it is your duty to discover how He sees you and what He wants for your life. Society loves to stereotype the role of a woman. Oftentimes these depictions end in the extremes. Either a woman should pit herself against men, trying to prove to society that she can stand in a man's world, or

We should celebrate our gender as a gift from God and not shirk our responsibility to excel in the role He designed for us

9 Exodus 35:30-35

women are encouraged to use their sexuality to accomplish what they want in life. Womanhood is neither. Using women as a sex symbol distorts God's ideals for women.

Manly Women was never God's design. Lesbianism is a female version of homosexuality and also sinful behavior. In Romans 1:25-27 NLT we read,

> *"That is why God abandoned them to their shameful desires. Even the women turned against the natural way to have sex and instead indulged in sex with each other. And the men, instead of having normal sexual relations with women, burned with lust for each other. Men did shameful things with other men, and as a result of his sin, they suffered within themselves the penalty they deserved."*

A gay and lesbian lifestyle is unnatural. It is against the grain of creation. It opposes God's original purpose and plan for humanity. These movements have become extremely militant to force-feed us with a homosexual agenda. They try their utmost to depict the unnatural as natural, the abnormal as normal. Anyone who takes a stand for Biblical truths and opposes the notion that homosexuality is normal behavior is coined a homophobic. It is interesting how a small percentage of society succeeds to intimidate the majority with this militant rhetoric. They silence voices of truth and dismiss the righteousness God has called for. A reversal of roles in gender is nothing but a rebellious stance against God's superior way of abundant living. It is demonically inspired to blatantly oppose Godly principles for successful living, stealing away our true identities forged by God. It is in these distorted relationships where natural procreation is impossible. These people revert to humanistic plans to creative pseudo family structures that cannot adequately support the beauty of God's blueprint for them.

A Womanly Woman is someone who stays in the role God cast for her. She is a woman in her core, beautiful and precious in God's sight. She is not man's maid or society's puppet. She embraces her God-given identity wholeheartedly and steps into all that God had planned for her. She is uniquely crafted and divinely resourced to impact her world. A Womanly Woman carries herself with confidence and finesse. Her inner beauty complements and directs her outer beauty. She personifies beauty instead of objectifying it. She refuses to become a sex symbol. She is deep and not shallow, sharp and not dull. She is delicate but strong and is no one's victim. She applies herself with dignity and models her life after God's purposes.

As Manly Men and Womanly Women we should celebrate our gender as a gift from God and not shirk our responsibility to excel in the role He designed for us. The most freedom a person can endure is to live within the Creator's personal and original design. Remember that the word "abuse" really means "abnormal use"? It stems from the idea that if an item is used beyond the perimeters of its original design it is being abused. For instance, when you use a ballpoint pen to poke a hole in a can, you are abusing the pen. It was not designed to poke holes in a can. If you instead write your name on a paper with that pen, you are using it according to its original design.

Abuse is dreadful and so many people are victims of it. They suffer at the hands of others. But when you willingly overstep God's original design perimeters for your life, or allow others to push you over those lines, then you are allowing abuse into your life. Gender abuse happens all the time and it can even be self inflicted. Stand up for who you are. Celebrate your manhood and womanhood by being a true Manly Man and Womanly Woman. Instead of seeking for reasons why bad things may have happened to you in the past, resolve in your heart not to look back but to reach forward. Do not try to right the wrongs of the past with yet another mistake. The gender rhetoric in the media today endeavors to normalize the abnormality of homosexuality, to make the unnatural natural. Do not get caught up in this deceptive and abusive form of life.

We were in a meeting in Ohio and Sharon was ready to minister to the people in song. While looking over the crowd of people in attendance, she saw two women sitting together. It was as if these two ladies stood out to Sharon and she knew the Lord wanted her to minister to them. In fact, at that moment the Lord gave Sharon a vision over their lives. She saw the Lord coming inbetween the two of them. We have never seen these ladies before and did not know their circumstances. Sharon ministered to them with a heart filled with love and compassion as she shared what the Lord had shown her. One lady was crying desperately while the other one was extremely angry. It looked like she was ready to attack my wife. After the meeting the pastors shared with us that these two ladies were involved in a lesbian lifestyle. They started to come to church because they wanted to expose their children to wholesome and godly education at the church. We returned to the same church about two years later. After the Sunday morning meeting a lady came to Sharon and said, "You probably do not recognize me." Sharon said, "We meet so many new people every week. Remind me who you are." The lady pulled out a picture and said, "This is what I looked like two years ago." She was that angry woman. She testified that her life was a mess at the time and she was a hurting, desperate woman clinging to anything that would help her feel loved and accepted. When Sharon said that the Lord was coming inbetween her and her lesbian partner, she was so mad. But that is exactly what happened. She said they simply drifted apart within a short time as God started to work on them. She said, "God transformed my life! He changed me emotionally,

The gender rhetoric in the media today endeavors to normalize the abnormality of homosexuality, to make the unnatural natural.

sexually, physically and professionally. She lost nearly 200 pounds in two years, without really trying. She found peace as God healed her emotional scars and wounds in her past. She was dating a wonderful man, completely and utterly in love and she was working as a principal in a nearby school for special needs children. The Lord turned her life around in a matter of months and she said she was happier than she could ever remember. The transformation was astounding! God stepped in and transformed a self absorbed, arrogant, angry lesbian into a beautiful, feminine, virtuous woman fully embracing God's divine design over her life. God helped her to discover His perfect plan and purpose for her life.

Another time while ministering in Ohio, Sharon saw a vision of an older man and a young man standing in front at the altar area of the church. These two men were not sitting together during the meeting, but God prompted her to call them out. As they stood next to each other in the front the Lord started to marvelously minister to them individually. The older man was crying as God revealed His awesome and unfailing love to him. It was as if God's love wrapped around this man where he was standing. We found out later that he was dying of AIDS and had never experienced genuine love in his life. He said he started to experience the power of God's love earlier in the meeting during worship. He was so touched by the presence of God. He had not cried for many years, but he felt something wet flowing over his face. He realized it was his own tears and he even wrote a note to thank Sharon and I for the word that was shared and for leading the people into such a deep time of worship into the very presence of God.

Returning to God's all natural way for living in relationships will return people to spiritual, emotional and greater physical health.

The younger man was also weeping. God's words to him were sterner and to the point, "You are playing with fire. Your life is on the line and I love you, but you are playing with fire." After the meeting the pastor seemed flabbergasted and summoned us to his office. He told us that no one really knew what just happened. These two men came to him in that week. They were living together and were in a homosexual relationship. They would get high on drugs and indulge in the lewdness of lust. The older man was indeed dying of AIDS, but the younger man had not contracted the decease yet. They came to the pastor because they wanted help to lead better lives. They came for prayer and counseling.

A year later, during another series of meetings at that church, we learned that the older man had since died. The younger man came up to Sharon and said, "I need to ask your forgiveness." Sharon asked, "What on earth for?" He said, "I heard what God was saying but did not heed the warning right away It took a few months for me to stop my sinful behavior and surrender my life to Christ fully. But I contracted AIDS and now have to live with this dreadful disease because of my stubbornness. Please forgive me." Sharon told him that she was not the one to ask for forgiveness. It was God who was the Source of that word and of the love that changed his life. That young man found peace, love, forgiveness and completeness in the hands and heart of Almighty God.

Back to the Natural

There is a great push today to get consumers back to an all natural diet. Dieticians and medical professionals agree that we should avoid processed foods as much as possible and go the organic, all natural route for healthier living. We think that approach should not stop with our choice in foods. Let's go all the way! Returning to God's all natural way for living in relationships will return people to spiritual, emotional and greater physical health. We need to identify the unnatural additives the enemy touts as ingredients that will bring greater happiness or quicker satisfaction for what they are. They produce fake freedom and imitation revelations and have destructive side effects. Let's not only focus on a holistic approach to food, but also to life. Nothing beats God's all natural ways! His is the best way to live and enjoy life.

Celebrate being a Manly Man and a Womanly Woman. In this day and age women tend to wear so many labels. Being a mom, carrier woman, homemaker and wife can wear you out. It is important to remember to be a Womanly Woman. The demands of everyday life can easily whittle away at your femininity. Take time to be a girl. Your husband will be the recipient of much pleasure as you put on your girly fragrance, wear your lacy lingerie and cute heels. Remind your husband that you are a sensual creature by being sensual towards him. Men, do not live in a man's world. Be a man in your wife's world. Display your virtues to the woman you love. Let her marvel at your muscles and hoot at your humor. Remind her of all the reason she loves you.

Prayer Application

Dear Heavenly Father
You do not make mistakes. You have marvelously made me. Help me to be a true representation of Your creation in me. Help me not to give into the interference and influence of others in my life. Satan wants to distort the perfection of Your plan. Show me how to live my life showcasing the Manly Man / Womanly Woman You delight in.
In Jesus name.
Amen.

Notes:

Mercurial Men And Whimsical Women

Every marriage should have a playful, spontaneous side to it. While marriage brings tremendous stability into your life because it anchors you and your better half to the potential of godly living, it also needs an element of surprise, intrigue and idealism. Marriage should have a fairytale element in the real world we live in, a "and they lived happily ever after" notion every day. Instead of wishing for a fairytale wedding, couples should aim for a fairytale marriage.

Predictability is not always required. Once righteous boundaries have been established around a married couple's lives, their canvas has been stretched and they can begin to paint on it. Color and texture can be applied to the canvas by adding detailed daily brush strokes, making their marriage uniquely personal.

We felt this chapter deserves a place in our book because in it we address the whimsical and mercurial side of a relationship. In a fairytale anything can happen. A fairytale has a good, uplifting story, is filled with all sorts of adventures, villains that plot evil plans are always defeated, characters have fun and break out in song every so often. Real world impossibilities become every day fairytale delights. Oh, and do not forget the element of love. Every good fairytale has a strong romantic overture. Did you know that Disney for the longest time refused to let a character die in one of their fairytales? Life endures in a fairytale and the ending is always sweet and happy.

There is no reason for your marriage not to have similar elements. Marriage is for grownups, but childlike moments are also important, where you can release your inner child to play with the love of your life in innocence and frivolity.[1] Far too many marriages end in divorce and not with a happily ever after. Our advice is simple: Make your marriage magical. Keep the romance going! You do not have to plan endless days of fairy-tale fun. Mere moments can be equally adventurous. Brush by your spouse with a whimsical swagger or give her the knight in shining armor look. Lean over to your man in a

Instead of wishing for a fairytale wedding, couples should aim for a fairytale marriage.

1 Frivolity means playfulness, lightheartedness, merriment, laughing and joking, giddiness.

crowded room and let him know in no uncertain terms your intentions for later that night. Develop your own exclusive love language others are oblivious to.

We often leave each other notes in unusual places. Sometimes these notes may only have one word on it, but the message may be a mouth full. Once I placed a note in the sugar canister for Sharon to find. I figured that when the sugar bowl is empty she would fill it from the canister and find the silly and somewhat naughty note. Well, the wife of our District Superintendent was helping Sharon in the kitchen one day. Her husband and I were visiting in the family room. He oversaw more than 100 churches at the time. The sugar bowl was empty and Sharon asked our guest to fill it up from the canister in the cupboard. Needless to say, she was surprised to find my note. Sharon quickly grabbed it and made it disappear while blushing for another 10 minutes. That night we laughed ourselves to sleep.

Another time, while I was on a missions trip Sharon had packed my bag and slipped naughty notes into pockets, my underwear and even my socks. Needless to say, I had a hard time disposing of the evidence so that my travel companions did not come upon them. It really blessed my heart and kept my mind on the love of my life. We frequently issue each other vouchers for a walk in the park, a kiss in the moonlight or a candlelit bath tub serenade.

Marriage should have plenty of room for the games we play, a place where we can be deliberately innocent and decidedly childlike. There is a big difference between being childlike and childish. Childishness is silliness. It speaks of immaturity and foolishness. Childlikeness is wholesome. It speaks of innocence, trusting and spontaneity. Childish refers to a person's behavior but childlike refers to a person's temperament. As adults we should not act childish. We are responsible human beings after all, but there is a playful child within us all.

Usually we hide that side of ourselves because it can make us vulnerable to the outside world. There is no better place to release your inner child than in marriage.

Whimsical Women

Women have a whimsical side to them. Being whimsical means to be amusing, playful and curious. The word even means to be spontaneous and fantastic. One definition states, "Whimsical is determined by change, impulse or whim rather than by necessity or reason"[2] Women are by far God's more fantastic creation. Men rarely can anticipate their every move. They are often unpredictable, playful and even mischievous. They love to be courted and romanced. Amidst our broken world their hearts are often idealistic. They are mood setters and moment capturers, longing for times of togetherness. They can turn grocery shopping into fellowship and a tennis match into a relational adventure. For them it is not about the stuff you do so much as who you do it with.

> **Marriage should have plenty of room for the games we play, a place where we can be deliberately innocent and decidedly childlike.**

Mercurial Men

Men are mercurial. To be mercurial means to be effervescent, buoyant, lighthearted, resilient, and changeable. Mercurial Men have effervescence in them. They are not like yesterday's coke in an open can. Life bubbles from their spirit and they cause dreams to float into the heart of their spouse. It is curious to see just how similar the words whimsical and mercurial are in meaning. One of the origins of mercurial comes from the element mercury or quicksilver. It is the only metal that is fluid at room temperature. It is a bad conductor of heat, but a great one for electricity. Mercury vapors are used in fluorescent lights to disburse light.[3] Mercurial Men stay cool

---

2 The Free Dictionary

3 Hammond, C. R. The Elements in Lide, D. R., ed (2005). CRC

and calm in a heated situation but provide light in the midst of darkness. They bring lightheartedness in a heavy-hearted situation. They are able to go with the flow, being spontaneous when needed.

The games we play are a natural part of our existence and some competition is even healthy. There is however a stark difference between being competitive and combative. Games ending in arguments speak of unresolved personal issues. It is part of marital playfulness to allow your spouse the odd win. Remember marriage is a partnership and team sport and when your spouse wins, you win. The two of you stand together. When you score your spouse scores! Keep your playfulness enjoyable. Balance stability with flexibility. Instead of wasting time trying to analyze and scrutinize your spouse to understand him or her, decide to flow with the love you have for him or her. Encourage an atmosphere of a fairy-tale ending everyday of your married life.

Handbook of Chemistry and Physics (86th ed.). Boca Raton (FL); CRC Press. ISBN 0-8493-0486-5

Prayer Application

Dear Heavenly Father
Help me to always see the brighter, cheerful things You have surrounded me with in my life. Your joy is my strength. Cause me to focus and meditate on the things that are true, noble, just, pure, lovely, of good report, things of virtue and praiseworthy. Let Your joy well up in me every day so I may be a wellspring and fountain of whimsy; quick to see the silver lining around every cloud and able to enjoy and share the lighter side of life with my spouse.
In Jesus name.
Amen.

Notes:

Chapter 12: Recovery

Melted Men And Wilted Women

Have you ever had your heart broken? Or have you ever been dealt a serious blow in life you thought you would not be able to recover from? Life can be very stressful. With responsibilities piled heavy upon husband's and wives' shoulders their knees often buckle, tempers flare up and their hearts are bruised. Even Mountain Moving Men might find a mountain too big to move and too high to climb. Wave Walking Women can encounter a wave too great to conquer. Sometimes it looks as if even great men and women are on the losing end of life's battles. Men are melting in the heat of battle while women are wilting in the midday sun. Men and women alike melt in the face of adversity and wilt by the scrutiny of the heat of their situations. What do you do when circumstances overwhelm you, when your cares and burdens out muscle your strength? You need relief from the heat, reprieve from situations and belief that all will be well.

Ordinary people have to deal with turbulent circumstances, the pain of divorce, the betrayal of adultery, inexcusable abuse and other conflict situations that produce immense emotional trauma. These are but a few situations that can cut deep furrows into a person's soul. No matter what life throws at you, you can be victorious! Regardless of the mistakes that have been made, you still have a chance to make things right. It may seem impossible for you but know that with God the impossibility becomes possible. What was once melted can be molded again and what was wilted can be revived again. You do not have to stand and accept the heartache the enemy has designed for you. Welcome and embrace the victory the Lord has destined for you.

The price tag of sin is always a price too high to pay. It kills life-dreams, happiness, aspirations, relationships, and holiness. It separates people from God and each other.

Melting & Wilting

When you melt as a man you feel separated. Your inner structure is changed, just like chocolate in the hot sun. You can cool down the chocolate after it was melted, but it will not quite be the same as before. The heat changed the chemistry of the candy bar. When you have reached your limit, totally overwhelmed in the heat of battle you lose control and melt and you fall apart.

A wilting woman is like a plant in the heat of the day. Moisture evaporates and the plant's leaves, petals and stems become limp and begin to wilt. Without the reintroduction of water, the plant will be permanently damaged or even die. Maybe you have experienced the onslaughts of life or the agony of adultery. Maybe you are amidst the anguish of abuse and your strength is all but gone. Is your spirit broken and are the flames of the furnace of life licking up your remaining moisture? When you move away from God instead of moving mountains with Him you start to melt and when you position your life in a scorching desert atmosphere instead of walking on water towards the Lord you start to wilt. Some battles are thrust upon you without your consent but sometimes you pick a wrong fight by stepping onto a battlefield that you should never have tread upon.

Bringing it on Yourself

David is a perfect example. He was supposed to be fighting with his men on the frontlines of honor against the Ammonites, but instead he faced a homegrown battle in his backyard.[1] It was springtime and the armies of God were poised to attack the armies of Ammon. David could have been the mighty king and commander in chief of Israel against the enemies of God but instead became a weak man, melting in the furnace of temptation. He should have been on the frontlines with his men strategizing but instead he retreated to the boredom of the palace. He focused on a beautiful married woman taking a bath instead of defending the honor and lives of his soldiers. After seducing Bathsheba he covered up his adultery by murdering her husband to take her for himself. She was pregnant with his baby. He was a melted man who allowed sin to change his moral fiber and bruise his spirit. Bathsheba was not an innocent bystander in all of this. She exposed herself out in the open for wandering, lustful eyes to see. She could have said no to the advances of David and refused to sleep

---

1 2 Samuel 11:1-27

with him, but she wilted in the heat of the moment. David was indeed looking down from the palace at a beautiful woman's body but Bathsheba looked up to the palace for the kings' attentions. Bathsheba was wilting in the heat of forbidden passion while David melted in the furnace of that same passion.

Sin has dreadful consequences. We read,

> *"For the wages of sin is death, but the free gift of God is eternal life through Christ Jesus our Lord."* [2]

The price tag of sin is always a price too high to pay. It kills life-dreams, happiness, aspirations, relationships, and holiness. It separates people from God and each other. Sin is personal but has a relational effect. David and Bathsheba paid a terrible price for their sin. The Bible says that "the Lord was displeased with what David had done."[3] Part of the consequences of David's sin was that his own household would rebel against him. What David had done in the privacy of the palace would happen to him in public view. We read in 2 Samuel 16:21-22 that Absalom, David's son, slept with David's concubines on the roof of the palace for all to see as an insult to his father. It did not end there. David and Bathsheba's child also died.[4] He describes the price of his sin,

> *"When I refused to confess my sin, my body wasted away, and I groaned all day long. Day and night your hand of discipline was heavy on me. My strength evaporated like water in the summer heat. Finally, I confessed all my sins to you and stopped trying to hide my guilt. I said to myself, "I will confess my rebellion to the LORD." And you forgave me! All my guilt is gone."* [5]

---

2 Romans 6:23 NLT

3 2 Samuel 11:27 NLT

4 2 Samuel 12:14-24

5 Psalm 32:3-5 NLT (For a full description of David's repentance

Thank God for the forgiveness of sin! God's forgiveness of sin is not His approval of that sin. The consequences of our personal sin are never just personal. It reaches further than us and affects those around us. The sin of adultery destroys not only the individuals involved, but also their families. David and Bathsheba were restored and in spite of this dreadful episode, although they had to bear the consequences and taste the bitterness that their adultery had produced – the loss of a child and effect on his family was no small price to pay. But David, after his restoration was described as a man after God's own heart.[6] They learned a great deal from their mistakes, and paid a terrible price, but they lived again. They emerged from the melting and wilting season stronger and with a new perspective on grace and forgiveness. Bathsheba bore him another son, Solomon, who would later become king of Israel in David's stead.

> **If you mess up, fess up. Your sin is no secret to God after all. The wonder of God is that He is poised and ready to forgive!**

Recovery

So how can one recover like David and Bathsheba? How do you turn towards recovery and away from the flames of circumstance? First you have to stop the melting mess and wilting woes in your life. According to David's account ignoring the problem is not an answer. Denial and silence actually allows the heat and pressure to increase. When he kept his sin to himself he suffered. His body wasted away and he groaned.[7] Did you know that spiritual and emotional distress can actually make you sick?

> *"For day and night thy hand was heavy upon me: my moisture is turned into the drought of*

---

read Psalm 51)

6 Acts 13:22

7 Psalm 32:3

summer" [8]

Scholars agree that the word used here for *"moisture"* actually can be translated *"life-blood"* and has to do with the marrow in your bones.[9] Marrow makes blood cells and platelets and helps prevent many deadly diseases. David's immune system was compromised because of his sin. He was melting away spiritually, physically and emotionally. So how did he stop that process? Well he confessed his mistakes to God and found forgiveness. Instead of hiding them he acknowledged them. He turned to God with a repentant heart. He did not have an "I'm sorry You caught me" attitude. He was truly ashamed and remorseful for what he had done. Stop keeping your sin a secret. If you mess up, fess up. Your sin is no secret to God after all. The wonder of God is that He is poised and ready to forgive! No matter what mistakes you have made, big or small, many or few, God will forgive you if you confess your faults. We read,

> *"If we confess our sins, He is faithful and just to forgive us our sins and to cleanse us from all unrighteousness."* [10]

Your road to recovery starts here with confession and repentance. Forgiveness follows and you are well on your way to be revived, refreshed and renewed. Now, remember even after forgiveness you probably still will face lingering consequences of your actions, but at least you will not be carrying the weight of them alone. God is with you. He carries you. He has forgiven you and lifted the burden of guilt, shame and regret from your shoulders and heart.

Being restored and renewed by the Lord will give you a second chance at fulfilling His original purposes for your life.

---

8 Psalm 32:4 KJV

9 A Hebrew and English lexicon of the Old Testament by Wilhelm Gesenius. page.527.

10 1 John 1:9 NKJV

Acknowledge God as your Shepherd, like David did in Psalm 23. Recognize that in Him you shall not want. Allow Him to lead you beside still waters and into green pastures. Let Him restore your soul and lead you along right paths that will bring honor to His name. He will anoint your head with oil and He will fill your cup once again to overflowing. He is beside you when you have to traverse deep dark valleys and He will take away your fear. He will be your Protector and He will bless and feed you even in the presence of your enemies. His goodness and mercy will pursue you instead of the ghosts of your past and you will experience His awesome presence in your life.

Forgiveness needs to flow on two levels. Initially it flows vertically, from the heart of God into your soul. Then it also needs to flow horizontally, from you to your spouse and vice versa. Unforgiveness breeds bitterness, resentment and other evil emotions. If Jesus forgives us of our sin, then we should follow His example. The Bible says,

> *"And judge not, and ye shall not be judged: and condemn not, and ye shall not be condemned: release and ye shall be released"* [11]

Remember, forgiveness does not flow in one direction. When you forgive, you are forgiven and when you release, you yourself are released. This is important even in abuse situations. Oftentimes abuse victims continue to harbor bitterness and resentment, anger and unforgiveness towards their aggressor. These very strong emotions wreak havoc on their souls and keep them in a state of continual brokenness, but with the aid of God they can step into the realm of forgiveness and be released of all these unholy emotions as well. Forgiveness is not overlooking or approving of what happened. It is merely placing that person into the hands of God instead of holding on to them yourself. It is a severing of destructive soul ties.

---

11 Luke 6:37 ASV

God knows how to deal with aggressors and He has better access to their souls than you do.

Time also helps to heal. In the heat of the moment you become weary and stressed out, but as time passes you gain better perspective and objectivity. We must stress however that putting time between you and your sin is not the solution. Restoration is activated through the forgiveness of sin.

Restoration is truly a beautiful thing! It returns furniture to their original condition and purpose. It also does the same with people. Being restored and renewed by the Lord will give you a second chance at fulfilling His original purposes for your life.

Being an Innocent Bystander

There are people who are melting and wilting because of circumstances beyond their control. Sometimes bad things happen to good people. Someone once preached a powerful sermon on restoration. He used the analogy of bread. One day Jesus took bread; He blessed it, broke it and shared it with the multitude as a blessing to them. Another day He took bread; blessed it, broke it and shared it with His disciples during the last Passover meal. A few days later, God took the Bread of Life, His only begotten Son; blessed Him, let Him be broken on the cross and shared Him with the world that whoever believed in Him should not perish but have eternal life! Now, let God take you in His hands. He will bless you. He sometimes also allows you to be broken so you too can share your victory with many others in search of victory in their own lives. A whole person that was broken and made whole again is in a great position to share the miracle of restoration to other broken people.

If you have been a victim of verbal abuse you are aware of the painful piercing of those destructive words discharged in heated arguments. These words fuel the fiery furnace of bitterness, resentment and even hate. It is important to consider the healing words of God and not to fall prey to the destructive words of man. Forgive and forget what was said. Renew your mind constantly, filling it with God's Word. This will inspire you to follow the truth and recover fully, not being melted or wilted by the lies spoken, but revived by the truth that God's Word alone can produce.

You live in a broken world and cannot always anticipate or prepare for destructive things that may happen to you, but you can control their effects on you. You can, through the help and power of God, rise up and be a blessing to those around you. When you are facing a fiery furnace because you stand up for what is right you will see victory amidst the flames. Think of Shadrack, Meshack and Abednego who faced peril and almost certain death simply because they would not worship an idolatrous statue of gold. When the heat was on the three of them, they sided with God and holy principles, even at the threat of being cast into a fiery furnace. Standing for what is holy and right is noble and righteous, but it does not always keep you out of the fire. If they had refused to bow, they would have faced the intense flames of the furnace. But if they had compromised their principles and worshipped the statue, they would have eventually had to endure the eternal flames of hell.

Do not move away from God. Move mountains with Him! And do not drown in the waves of your circumstances, walk on them to victory!

Sometimes you have to go through a fiery furnace. You have to endure some heat, but remember what happened to the three friends. They were bound and thrown in the fire, but while in the fire they were unbound and encountered God.[12] God literally stepped into the fire with them. Witnesses from the outside saw four men instead of three in the fire! What started out as a test and challenge became an encounter and springboard to promotion and honor. Face your challenges

12 Daniel 3:25

today with faith and perseverance. Expect encounters with Almighty God during your trial and believe that you too will find measured freedom from the bonds of the past. If God did it for Shadrack, Mesack and Abednego, He will surely do it for you too.

Emerging Victoriously

You can come out of the fire not only intact, but also stronger and blessed. Take responsibility for your actions. Instead of reacting to outside pressure, interferences and circumstances, take the initiative in your life. Decide to forgive and release. Refuse to be bound by the accusations and words of man. Invite the Lord into your fiery furnace. Give Him the opportunity to step along side you to lead you victoriously through and marvelously out. You need God's perspective. He is for you and not against you. Do not allow self pity to govern your mind. If you have been melted because of the fiery words of others, you need to focus on the Word of God instead. If you have been wilted by extreme circumstances, then take your stance on the Word of God and allow Him to step in. Apply His words to your life in a personal way.

> *"When you pass through the waters, I will be with you, and through the rivers, they will not overwhelm you. When you walk through the fire, you will not be burned or scorched, nor will the flame kindle upon you."* [13]

Do not give up, get up! Endure to the very end. Change what you can and leave the rest up to God. Remember who you are! You are a Mountain Moving Man and a Wave Walking Woman. You have the ability to do the impossible together with God. Let go of the hurt of yesterday and be planted, rooted and grounded by God. Place yourself in His hands and you'll be secure no matter what. You'll emerge from your trial victoriously.

---

13 Isaiah 43:2 AMP.

Do not move away from God. Move mountains with Him! And do not drown in the waves of your circumstances, walk on them to victory!

Prayer Application

Dear Heavenly Father
Help me to see that with You by my side I can do all things. You are Healer. Deliver me from the past hurts and mistakes that has wilted my spirit and caused my strength to melt away. I pray that You form and fashion me again. Restore my soul and allow me to see Your plan and purpose for my life come to be.
In Jesus name.
Amen.

Notes:

Chapter 13: Promotion

Marketing Men And Wholesale Women

Marketing Men and Wholesale Women understand the importance of investments and the value of treasure. They are not traders but investors, unwilling to relinquish their most precious investment in this lifetime. They have an eye to spot areas of potential and gain within the scope of their spouse's soul. They fiercely defend each other's honor and protect each other's integrity.

Your spouse is a resource you want to own stock in. In fact, their value will increase year after year and you want to buy into and not sell from their worth at any time. Yes, buy shares in each other because the dividends are incomparable with any other investment you can ever make on earth. Marriage is all about sharing. It is about sharing life together. There is however no room for trading on a marital stock exchange. Someone else's spouse cannot be traded for your own because that is adultery. You cannot share yourself with someone other than your spouse in what can be described as a competitive market. That is adultery too. Do not bankrupt your marriage! The better stock option is already in your marriage portfolio! The only selling you should ever do is selling out to God together. His long term investments are the most profitable. With Him your eternal retirement is secure, your short term prosperity assured and your medium outlook a blissful marriage with the person you love.

Marketing Me

Advertisements and promotions has become the bedrock of commercial endeavors. Good advertising means greater profits. It affects the bottom line. Too many people have taken principles of product marketing and recklessly applied them to promote themselves. Their attitude is "do whatever you can as long as it takes care of the bottom line." Principles and integrity have fallen out of favor and have been replaced with a competitive mind-set and hostile takeover mentality. Even in marriage spouses oftentimes jostle for prominence among themselves. They sell or promote themselves often using tactics that hurt the opposing party.

Stop trying to sell yourself. The problem is that you will have difficulty determining your own value.

The Bible has a much better way to get ahead in life.

> *"A man's gift makes room for him, and brings him before great men."*[1]

This is a powerful verse with a dual meaning. God has blessed each person with gifts and abilities they excel in, natural and spiritual gifts that when applied in life will open tremendous doors of opportunity in a person's life. In effect, you are a gift that will gain access and excel when you apply yourself in accordance to the purposes and plans God has for your life.

Self promotion is overrated when it comes to marriage. While confidence is a good quality, you should always trust in the gifts God placed in you to propel you forward. Apply your gifts every day and God will show you the way. Create room for yourself in your spouse's heart by using your talents and gifts to bring honor and glory to the Lord in your marriage.

Stop trying to sell yourself. The problem is that you will have difficulty determining your own value. Either you are going to sell yourself short resulting in sickening inferiority or you will oversell your worth ending in nauseating pride. We have seen couples opposing each other as if they are competing for the same market share. Each spouse vying for a better position, especially when it comes to the perception of others. They run opposing advertising campaigns, promoting their own strengths and alerting the public of the potential flaws of their partner, with great finesse and subtlety of course. This is no way to do marriage! Such behavior is destructive.

Nothing will make the stock market of your life crash quicker than jealousy. It is a very destructive thing. We read in God's Word,

> *"For wherever there is jealousy [envy] and contention [rivalry and selfish ambition], there will*

---

1 Proverbs 18:16 NKJV

also be confusion [unrest, disharmony, rebellion] and all sorts of evil and vile practices." [2]

If running your spouse or others down makes you feel better about yourself, then you have a problem with self worth and you should revisit our chapter on Molded Men and Woven Women and realize your God given uniqueness. Jealousy invades the soundest investment deeming it insecure and vulnerable. Whether common jealousy or spousal jealousy, they are both equally destructive and affect not just your life but the lives of others around you. Jealousy breeds confusion and disharmony. The Bible teaches us to celebrate with the victory of others. God *"resists the proud and gives grace to the humble."*[3] Some people are filled with jealousy when they see others excel in certain areas of giftedness. Maybe you do not have a great singing voice but you bake a mean chocolate cake. Do not fixate on your inability to sing but rejoice in your baking proficiency. We have met individuals that are so insecure about themselves because they project and profess to be like others or are threatened by the gifts of others. May your ears be blessed by melodious singing and your tummy by delicious chocolate cake! Maybe you are good with arranging numbers but challenged with relating to people, then rejoice that your spouse takes the lead in establishing and maintaining your circle of friends while you administrate your monthly budget and financial obligations.

Sometimes people are inspired by a charismatic leader or influential individual and they would start to mimic that person on different levels. They would adapt their lifestyle to look like or act like the person they admire. While this may be harmless at first glance and flattering to the leader involved, it could also lead to an altering of the essence and worth that God has uniquely gifted you with. Be yourself and do not sell out to be someone else. Do not follow trends and popularity pursuits

---

2 James 3:16 AMP.

3 1 Peter 5:5

but follow God. True leaders will encourage principle replication that does not destroy individualism. What seems so innocent in just wanting to look like someone or be inspired by them can also change into jealousy and envy that adds unintended pressures to you, your spouse and your marriage and lead to greater comparisons in more areas of your life. Think of it as a self imposed tax that drains the stockpiles of blessings from your marriage, reducing its net worth in your mind.

Do not compare your strengths with the weaknesses of your spouse. Stop using false advertisement to gain a greater share of life's limelight from your spouse. Be honest with yourself and with God about who you are and who you are married to. Competitiveness in sports and games is one thing, but it does not belong in your marriage relationship. Do not trash the concept of marriage but be a poster child for it. Marriage is a co-op[4] not a coop. It is an institution designed by God for the mutual benefit of both the husband and wife.

When your actions serve to bring blessing to God, they will also bring blessing to your spouse. Remember he or she is God's gift to you.

You do not have to prove yourself to anyone. God made you and if you will allow Him to show you who He made you to be, you will discover tremendous gifts in yourself that you have at your disposal to step through the doors of success with your spouse. Your gifts will sell themselves. You should be uniquely you.

What if others are blind to the strengths you possess? Sometimes you may feel like people and even your spouse fail to see the true qualities that you have. Such feelings are attached to your own insecurity. Only God can uncover and disclose the market place of your life and the warehouse of wholesale

4 A Co-op or cooperative is a business organization owned and operated by a group of individuals for their mutual benefit.

blessings stored up in your spirit. Positioning yourself in the light of God these characteristics will be illuminated and you will not feel the need to push those around you into the shadows so you can enjoy the attention. A great compliment to you is when you can share the spotlight with your spouse or even push your spouse into a place of prominence. After all, your life partner is your better half and God's gift to you. You both belong in the spotlight of God's love together.

Representations

You do not represent yourself. You are an ambassador firstly of God and secondly of your spouse. Your life revolves around bringing honor to God in everything you do. The Bible teaches us,

> *"And whatever you do, do it heartily, as to the Lord and not to men."* [5]

When your actions serve to bring blessing to God, they will also bring blessing to your spouse. Remember he or she is God's gift to you. What you do and say reflects on your spouse and represents him or her. How you look and what you wear should not be targeted for the eyes of others. You should be eye candy to your spouse. Your image is important. A hot or sexy look makes you an advertisement that will attract unwanted buyers or borrowers when you are not for sale. It is nothing more than a selfish look. There is nothing wrong with looking great for your spouse, even hot and sexy for him or her, but remind yourself that it is for him or her. Remember you are not selling yourself you are already sold out to God and to your spouse. Someone once said. "If you live close to God and His infinite grace, you do not have to tell, it shows on your face."

You do not represent yourself. You are an ambassador firstly of God and secondly of your spouse.

5 Colossians 3:23 NKJV

Promotion

Spouses promote each other. They are a resource for each other strengths. One may be good in the kitchen and the other in finances. Recruit your spouse to strengthen your weaknesses. When you struggle with something that your spouse might excel in, then embrace and celebrate their expertise and welcome their capability. Let your spouse fill in your gaps. If your spouse does extremely well in an area, then promote, encourage and steer them towards that strength. In effect you are promoting God's gifts and talents in them.

When we got married I was already well aware of the amazing musical talents and spiritual anointing the Lord has placed into Sharon's life. Even at our wedding the Lord reminded us of His mandate on our lives. We were to usher in His glory wherever we would go. He was going to establish us as a ministry team. I realized that what the Lord placed in us, but especially in her, was special and the enemy would try his level best to bury these gifts under tons of trash. It was my duty not to aid him in his evil plots but to help my sweetheart to delve for gold in her, unearthing the very gifts that have shaped her life and our ministry.

In the early years of our marriage in South Africa there were very few anointed female ministers she could model after. Women could not be ordained at the time. It was a season in which the Church was grappling with how to handle gifts while maintaining doctrinal integrity. Sharon oftentimes was reduced to baking cakes, and catering for weddings and funerals as the primary expression of ministerial work. We both knew her calling was not to fill people's bellies, but their souls. I shared in her frustrations and together we waited on the Lord for His direction. Over the next few years He took us both on a great adventure of discovery, often reminding us that we are a ministry team and should stand together while exploring all avenues to usher in God's glory in the best possible ways. Sharon felt the pressure of breaking old ministry molds and traditional mind-sets while pursuing her gifting to bring honor to the Lord.

I had to make a determined decision to push her forward and to protect her from religious spirits and ignorant people. Even today we have a standing agreement in meetings that she has full freedom to flow with what God shows her, no matter when or where and I will support her fully and vice versa. We flow as a team and go to great lengths to protect the fibers of unity that keeps us functioning as one. This unity does not come automatically. You have to work at it and protect it continually.

Many times the Lord would use the spiritual gifts He placed in Sharon to open powerful ministry doors for our lives. She would be invited to sing at an event or to lead worship. The power of God would descend on the meeting and open the hearts of key leaders to invite us back. In meetings we see this every week. Sharon would flow in song or prophecy, opening the hearts of people, preparing them for the power of the proclamation of the word of God. Altars would fill up with hungry souls connecting to God in an atmosphere of spiritual intensity.

Sharon often says that she would never have done what she did if it was not for the anointing of the Lord and the encouragement of her husband. I wholeheartedly say the same about my ministry accomplishments. She is a driving force that pushes me beyond the boundaries of past limitations, showing me ways to activate the anointing of the Holy Spirit to accomplish what I never thought I could. When I preach, she is my biggest cheerleader, sitting on the front row enthusiastically listening and actively engaged in what God has called me to do. She encouraged me to study, to write and to develop my gifts in life. Sometimes she'll come up with a great idea and I'll find a way to make it happen; to give feet to a vision.

Rudi has been my mentor in ministry. I've learned to study

the Word, to delve in the original languages and look at God's word with a prophetic mind-set, all because of his encouragement and example. He has pushed me beyond what I thought would be possible. He is a constant student, always learning and studying with a mentality to make things that need to be done, happen, even if he needs to learn to do it himself. I have a tremendous respect for my husband because even in tough situations he stays ahead of the curve and anticipates our next move with a prophetic eye on the future and his ears tuned to the Lord's voice. I am his help whenever and wherever he needs it.

When we speak words of life over each other they activate the seeds of God's Word buried deep within us to reach our full potential in Him.

Together we promote each other to the glory of God. When we speak words of life over each other they activate the seeds of God's Word buried deep within us to reach our full potential in Him. In marriage we found a dynamic partnership, reinforced by our mutual faith in God.

We are constantly aware of the fact that without the anointing of the Lord we would be nowhere near where He has brought us. After all Jesus declared,

> *"I am the Vine and you are the branches, if I am in you and you are in Me you will bear much and abundant fruit, however apart from Me you can do nothing."* [6]

May our personal testimony inspire you to identify and activate God's gifts and the potential He has placed in you. Inspire, encourage and admonish each other.

---

6 John 15:4 AMP.

Prayer Application

Dear Heavenly Father
You are the Promoter in my life. Thank you that You open doors of blessing and opportunity for me. May I ever represent You in all I do. Cause me to reflect Your image for the world to see my life is modeled after Thee. Help me to be a good steward of all You have given me because You determine my worth.
In Jesus name.
Amen.

Notes:

Chapter 14: Discovery

Menu Gazing Men And Window Shopping Women

We are dedicating part of this chapter to the precious folks still looking for their better half. We want to share some powerful principles that will guide you through this very important process. There are so many people in the world, each one with special qualities, unique strengths and weaknesses. Choosing the right spouse is paramount in your life. In fact, it is so important that you simply cannot afford to keep God out of the process. Too many well meaning people simply surrender the responsibility of this choice to an internet website or dating service. They abdicate a big portion of their accountability to complete strangers, pay a "finder's fee" to get access to a huge list of prospective spouses and hope for the best. We believe it to be the duty of every believer to incorporate God in the process of finding His perfect spouse for your life.

In the chapter, Molded Men and Woven Women, we saw that God has molded and woven you with His purposes in mind. Your search should start here, with God. Jesus said,

> *"But seek first the kingdom of God and His righteousness, and all these things shall be added to you."* [1]

Where to look?
The Bible is very clear,

> *"Ask, and it shall be given to you; seek and you will find; knock and it will be opened to you."* [2]

Ordering a spouse from a bar menu or shopping for one online is not a perfect place to start. Become a Menu Gazing Man and a Window Shopping Woman to find Mr. or Mrs. Right. Having your eyes, the windows of your heart, solely fixed on Jesus will bring illumination to the correct choices of character or ingredients for a choice spouse.

Ordering a spouse from a bar menu or shopping for one online is not a perfect place to start. Become a Menu Gazing Man and a Window Shopping Woman to find Mr. or Mrs. Right.

---

1 Matthew 6:33 NKJV
2 Matthew 7:7 NKJV

Allow us to share our personal experience when it comes to seeking and finding the right life partner.

One day, before I met Rudi I was ordering a chicken and mayonnaise sandwich at Wimpy Burger, a well known South African franchised restaurant. I remember being very hungry while I placed my order and could feel my taste buds salivate. I was on my lunch break and could already taste my favorite sandwich even before I took the first bite. I was specific in ordering to make sure the restaurant would get my delicious order just the way I liked it. While standing at the counter waiting on my order, the Lord started to speak to me. He said, "If only you had faith in Me when you pray like you trust this server to get your order right. I have the best in store for you. You can trust Me, even in finding the best husband for you." I was struck in my heart and realized my level of unbelief and doubt. God was addressing my lack of trust. I felt the conviction of the Holy Spirit as He addressed my own unbelief and repented. That very night, during my quiet time I explored the Scriptures to confirm what I believed was the voice of God speaking to me. To my amazement I came across Matthew 7:9-11 as well as Luke 11:11-13.[3] I had heard these verses before, but never had they been as clear as that night in my room. Luke 11:12–13 references three food items namely bread, fish and an egg. Note that Jesus was not referring to food in general, but He was instructing us to be specific in prayer. Something leaped in my spirit as I realized the Lord was clearly telling me to "Look at the menu" and order myself a husband to my liking. God was saying He is better than the best waiter on earth and more than able to answer my prayers in a way that will exceed my expectations.

---

3 Luke 11:11-13 NKJV *"If a son asks for bread from any father among you, will he give him a stone? Or if he asks for a fish, will he give him a serpent instead of a fish? Or if he asks for an egg, will he offer him a scorpion? If you then, being evil, know how to give good gifts to your children, how much more will your heavenly Father give the Holy Spirit to those who ask Him!"*

I started to read Psalm 139 and I realized how He uniquely knit me together in my mother's womb. He knew me before I even took my first breath. He wrote down the days of my life. He knows my beginning and end. That's when I really got excited. You see I had already memorized Jeremiah 29:11. His plans and my days were going to be wonderful because I belonged to Him. I was energized in this new knowledge. God wanted the best for me. I heard Him say it time and time again, "Sharon, do not settle for second best, I have the best in store for you." While activating my faith to have a new level of confidence in Him when I prayed, God wanted me to disclose to Him the desires of my heart, not in generalities, but being specific about just what I like. I was placing my order at God's restaurant and He was not going to disappoint me with the results!

I hope you are inspired by my testimony so far. God has His best in store for you too! Find out what dish is your favorite and then order it! The Lord directed me to ask Him for a husband and to be specific about it. My first reaction was that I did not really know what I would like in a husband. So the Lord said to me, "Look at the menu." I started to make a list. Walking about town, I would see a young man on the street and would say, "Lord, I like this about him, but not that; keep the looks but lose the personality, and so on." Item number one on my list was for him to be a man of God, wholly devoted to the Lord." I went into quite a lot of detail and asked for him to be tall dark and handsome. As my list grew, my faith grew along with it. I was constantly in conversation with God about my husband-to-be. I even shared with my coworkers what I was requesting from God in prayer. Some laughed and said, "We wanted the same and just got the opposite." I quickly responded, "But you did not pray for your husbands, I am and God will give me the desires of my heart." During this time I also prayed for my future husband. Although I had not met Rudi yet, I was asking the Lord to bless him wherever he was, to make his ways prosperous and if he was seeing another girl to cut off that relationship and keep him for me!" Rudi often quips that there was a season in his life girls thought he had leprosy or something contagious and would have nothing to do with him. God was at work and answering my prayer. Thank God, because he was quite a catch.

All the while one of my Bible School friends called me. "Rudi, I need your help" he explained. During our vacation breaks he usually took evangelism teams to different cities in South Africa. One of the team leaders pulled out and my friend asked me to take his place. I gladly accepted his invitation and changed my vacation plans accordingly. I had one day to prepare and pack. I was assigned to the Free State town of Welkom, in the heart of South Africa's agricultural and mining districts. My team consisted of 12 girls and 3 guys, including me. We arrived on Sunday morning and we planned to attend the church service that night before hitting the streets on Monday, declaring Jesus to everyone we would encounter.

On Sunday evening, when we walked into the church, we found seats near the front. I spotted Sharon as she was playing trumpet in the church band, and she saw me leading this group of girls and a couple of guys to our seats. I noticed her immediately and thought she looked terrific while blowing her trumpet in Zion. I think my heart was beating louder than the bass drum that night. Later on she told me that when she saw me she said, "Lord, I like that!" After the meeting, she invited my group to join their youth group at the coffee bar they used as an evangelistic outreach center in town. (Coincidentally she also initiated the outreach ministry among the young adults in her church.) We spoke but a few sentences that day, but Sharon went home and told her mom that she had met her husband! I also knew that she was the one for me.

I was placing my order at God's restaurant and He was not going to disappoint me with the results!

It was love at first sight. We loved everything we saw in each other. There was a definite spark that ignited a fire in our hearts for each other that is still burning strong today. "Mom, I'll faint if he kisses me!" Sharon and her mother laughed together over a hot cup of tea. We were attracted to each other in no uncertain terms. We wanted to be together, sharing every moment to get to know each other. We were like two students working together in the chemistry lab! Each brought a special, unique blend of ingredients that were blended together into a marvelous love relationship. I remember thinking, "Rudi, she's the one. All you have to do now is to convince her, and you have one week to do it."

That week turned out to be a week of destiny for us. While we enjoyed every moment together we also enjoyed God's presence together in church. It turned out that not only were we attracted to each other, but also to Jesus, our Lord and Savior and serving Him together was going to be adventurous to say the least.

You need to raise the bar when it comes to looking for the right spouse.

God fulfilled every line item on Sharon's list. It was truly uncanny! He left nothing out. He even showed me things she asked Him to reveal to me about her that no other person knew. The Bible says clearly,

> *"Delight yourself in the Lord, and He shall give you the desires of your heart."* [4]

And,

> *"Trust in the Lord with all your heart, and lean not on your own understanding. In all your ways acknowledge Him and He shall direct your path."* [5]

---

4 Psalm 37:4 NKJV
5 Proverbs 3:5-6 NKJV

Sharon and I have shared this testimony many times to many people. Several made up their own lists and started to pray that the Lord would lead them to the right life companion. Some even showed up in one of our meetings to introduce us to the answer to their prayer. If you are still looking for a life partner, go ahead, make your list. Make it a matter of prayer. God placed in you desires, likes, needs and wants that is unique. But He also made someone for you that would be a perfect person to meet those needs, fulfill your desires and be the person you would want to spend the rest of your life with. Do not settle for just anyone. God wants to give you the best. Place your order, activate your faith and keep the flame burning in you with prayer and expectation.

If you already placed your order, and your meal was delivered to your table, stop looking at the menu. Your food is getting cold. Start enjoying the chef's creation! He knows your palette and taste.

Menu Gazing Men need to know that God is a master chef that only uses organic, wholesome and healthy ingredients to create the answer to your prayer. Every meal is made to order and made fresh every time. He never serves substandard food or uses ingredients past their expiration dates. His pantry is fully stocked.

You need to raise the bar when it comes to looking for the right spouse. Identify the ingredients displayed in the life of a prospective spouse. Bitter ingredients will not produce a sweet marriage. Unresolved past issues will not simply evaporate after marriage. Make sure neither you nor your prospective spouse bring any unnecessary baggage into your marriage. Deal with things before and not after, sooner rather than later. Remember hurting people hurt people but healed people heal people.

Whose kitchen are you ordering from? The bar's menu is limited. They do not specialize in food but in drink. Marriage material is not found everywhere. Marriage is not fast food, it is fine dining. Marry up, not down. The Bible says, *"Taste and see that the Lord is good."*[6] God wants you to, *"ask and you shall receive."*[7] Entrust God with all the details, qualities and ingredients about your future spouse. Let your marriage be God made and not man-made.

Window Shopping Women identify the qualities of a quality product. Whose name is attached to the product? Who is the manufacturer? Can you see the craftsmanship of God in their lives? When it comes to shopping for a life partner, you want to look through the right windows. Every year thousands of people cannot wait to go window shopping at the famous department stores in New York. These stores are not bargain barns and certainly not cheap, but they carry quality merchandise. What are the qualities you are looking for in a man? Remember, online shopping has its risks. You cannot rely on a stranger's opinion to produce a perfect partner for you. Online dating sites can be prone to false advertising. People tend to list only positives and not negatives. Porn sites portray second hand items. Do not shop at a garbage dump but rather go to a jewelry store to find your jewel. When you find your covering then wear him with dignity and pride. Stop shopping around for someone better.

A Menu Gazing Man or Window Shopping Woman who is looking for that perfect spouse who will complete your life is on a great adventure that will change the direction and purpose of your life. Do not embark on this adventure in haste or desperation. Stay sober and vigilant. Do not be led by your emotions, but rather let you emotions be led by the Holy Spirit. Do not see yourself as the one on the shelf, as the article that is for sale. Do not let others shop for you. Ask the Lord to lead

---

6 Psalm 34:8

7 Matthew 21:22; Mark 11:24; John 16:24 and Matthew 7:7

you on this quest and follow His treasure map for the husband or wife you deserve.

Prayer Application

Dear Heavenly Father
You have designed my life and want the best for me. Open my eyes to the wonders of Your handiwork in others so I can see what You want for me. Help me to be true to the choice I make. And may my first choice be to follow You with my whole being. No compromise in value's and virtues. Your word has stated that I must ask of You and make my requests known to You, Lord. I now open up all I am and in transparency I lay my heart's desires before you. Let Your will be done in me and Your Kingdom come. Rule my life as the King of my Heart.
In Jesus name.
Amen.

Notes:

Chapter 15: Ten Secrets to Success

Magnificent Men And Wonderful Women

In this chapter we are sharing our 10 Secrets to a great marriage. We look at how to activate the magnificence in your man and the wonderful in your woman.

We were on a flight one night from Atlanta on our way to a ministry venue in Philadelphia. We were invited to speak at a marriage seminar. The flight attendant came to our seats with his usual offer of peanuts and soda, and then asked us a startling question, "Are you guys on honeymoon?" He saw how in love we are and needed a reason why. Sharon laughed and said, "Yes, we have been married for 20 years and are still on honeymoon!" The man was flabbergasted. He replied, "My marriage lasted only 8 years, what is your secret to having such a great marriage?" During the flight we pulled out a pen and paper and brainstormed to come up with our 10 secrets for a great marriage. We shared it with the flight attendant when we arrived at the airport and he thanked us profusely. These are but 10 of many principles we apply to our marriage and we have enjoyed the blessings attached to all of them. Allow us to share them now with you too.

Married life is exclusive and not inclusive. Do not allow outside interference to muddle it.

1. God First

Place God first in your life. Let Him take the lead in all areas of your life. Place Him above all else and include Him in all your life decisions. He'll guide you towards happiness, success and abundance.

2. Give 100% of yourself to your spouse

Marriage is not a 50/50 deal. When you give 100% of yourself to it along with your spouse, then you have 200% to work with instead of only 100% to make your marriage great! You'll start in abundance and not lack. In marriage you cannot afford to hold even a fraction back. Pour yourself wholeheartedly and completely into each other.

3. No Secrets

Transparency is very important in marriage. It speaks of trust.

With it you can turn your back and your spouse can still see what you are up to. The only secrets you should allow in your heart are those you and spouse carry together. Establish sacredness to your marriage that is exclusively yours. We share computer passwords and bank accounts and have access to all e-mail and Facebook accounts. We have no hidden things period.

4. Build a new life together

Married life is exclusive and not inclusive. Keep your parents, friends and coworkers out of your marriage. Do not allow outside interference to muddle it. Build a new life with your spouse, tailor-made to meet your needs and fit your lives with God. Including God in it is not outside interference. He is already in your hearts, remember? As a rule you simply cannot run to outsiders every time you face a challenge, but you should run to God every day. If you invite outside help with a specific situation it should be endorsed by both spouses and only someone qualified to help with that situation. This excludes personal sympathizers who'll only "gang" up against your spouse to make you feel better.

Be prepared for a new circle of friends. The old boys night out and girl's night out is no longer desirable within marriage context. From now on you do things together.

5. Honor, Respect and Protect

You should esteem your spouse higher than yourself. Treat them with the respect and honor you want to be treated with. Remember your spouse is God's precious gift to you. Your actions towards each other should be respectful, uplifting and encouraging to one another. Know each other's trigger points and respect your spouse's vulnerabilities. Protect them in those areas. Instead of exposing them to ridicule, strengthen them in grace. Respect them privately and publicly. As your spouse they deserve your best. Secure them in your love.

6. Keep sex an adventure

Do not be afraid to explore new adventures with your spouse in the bedroom, or any room for that matter. When you apply pure principles, without introducing perversions of sexuality like pornography, etc., to your intimacy, you can enjoy it with your spouse as God's gift to you. Keep such moments as sacred secrets between the two of you. Such adventures have no place in common chatter with others.

7. Pray together

Prayer is a visible expression of your connection to God. When you pray together you remind yourselves that you are building your lives around Almighty God and that He is important in your lives. You have a sure foundation to build your marriage upon. This is a great way to refresh and refocus your relationship with each other after having a disagreement. Prayer brings God into your situation and clears the air in your relationship of all the unholy emotional pollutants. It will replenish your love for each other just like the scent of fresh air after a rain. Forgiving and forgetting is sealed in God's presence and will accelerate the replenishing of joy and peace in your lives. Of course, prayer should not only be reserved for an emergency. Daily thankfulness together keeps life's focus where it should be, squarely on God.

8. Make time for each other

Your most valuable asset in life is the time the Lord gave you. The way you spend your time will determine so many things in your life. Spending quality time with your spouse is a priority. Your time-investment with him or her will yield amazing long-term results. Do adventures together. Participate in your spouse's favorite activities. If she likes to shop, go shopping with her and do not leave your best attitude at home. Remember you are there to share time with her. If he loves golf, go with him, and if you cannot golf, volunteer to drive the cart for him every now and then. Make him feel like a pro, even when his inner golfing skill decides not to cooperate with his outer performance. If you spend as much time with each other now as you did during your courtship, most marriage issues will be automatically resolved. Keep your pursuit for each other going.

Reinstitute date night. Yes, go out on a date every so often. You can be creative to fashion date night to stay interesting, fresh and fun. Do not get stuck in a rut by doing the same thing all the time. Make turns to plan date night, but get it on the calendar and make it a regular feature on your schedule. It should fit your budget and need not be an expensive endeavor. Date night need not always be at night time. Take a stroll together in your favorite park. Pack a picnic basket. Meet at the games arcade for lunch, or learn to play tennis together. The activity is secondary to simply spending time with the one your love. Make a coupon good for a long kiss on the couch or relaxing massage. Include an expiration date which will force your spouse to cash in on the action quick. Another great inexpensive date night might include a stroll in the moonlight, a relaxing foot massage and candle lit bathtime bubbles. Use your own imagination to create unforgettable moments together.

Your words are seeds planted in the seedbed of your spouse's heart. Seed will always yield a harvest so make sure you use good seed and not bad seed.

9. Communicate

Do not think it, speak it! Good communication is vital to a good marriage. Your words are seeds planted in the seedbed of your spouse's heart. Seed will always yield a harvest so make sure you use good seed and not bad seed. If you sow weeds into your spouse by being negative or amplifying their flaws with your words, guess what will grow even more abundant in them? But if you sow good, uplifting and encouraging things in them, guess what will grow in them? Words are powerful. They have limiting as well as freeing ability. Remember, you are what you speak. Start to invest in your spouse's future. Do your part to speak life over them instead of death, good instead of bad, encouragement instead of discouragement. You will eat the very fruit your words will produce in them.

But not all communication is verbal. Show your spouse how much you love them. Your posture towards them is important. Your actions in their lives will speak louder than you words in the ears.

When you speak out against your spouse you are doing two things that will harm your marriage. First, you are sowing the wrong seed with your words. Secondly, you are bringing in a third party into your marriage duet. Mouthing off about your spouse to someone else paints a distorted picture of your most precious treasure that will outlast any conflict, magnify your negative mind-set and prevent simple solutions to complex problems. Poking holes in your covering or carrier causes you to leak too. Do not share your offense with another and refuse to carry someone else's offense on your heart. If you had a disagreement with your spouse and you run to a friend or family member to garner support for your point of view, and after a while, love rules and you make up with your spouse and love them even more, that third party is still seething through their teeth at your spouse. Their relationship with your better half is strained and you wonder why? You painted the picture of your spouse in their minds. You brought them into a place in your marriage that they should not have access to.

When you are in a mood do not brood. Snap out of it!

Words are construction workers. They build and tear down, create and destroy. Do not use your tongue as a wrecking ball against your spouse but rather as a construction team that builds a masterpiece right before your eyes.

Good vertical communication with God will enhance horizontal communication with your spouse. Learn to open up to Him and you'll find it easier to open up to your spouse. The closer you get to God the closer you will get to each other.

Another way to cultivate and enhance your communication is to ask your spouse about their thoughts on different topics. What they think of the news, weather and current events. Do not stop to inquire from them. Do not act as if you already know them, but let them express their thoughts personally. Check in with each other daily. Inquire about their needs and make your "to do" lists adventurous. After you have done things together, initiate rewards. Make a point of asking your spouse about things that is not connected to work or tasks at hand. Make chit chat a priority. Many relationships become fatigued in communication because they reduce their words about work, children and the tasks at hand. Talk about the lighter things of life as well. Do not allow your smart-phone, I-Pod and I-Pad to infringe upon your one on one time with your spouse. Make your spouse a priority above your technology.

10. Don't be mad be glad.

When you are in a mood do not brood. Snap out of it! The longer you spend thinking about a given situation or the neglect of your spouse, the deeper this negative emotion settles in and the longer it will take to get it out. Find ways to dismantle the explosive situations. Divert anger with humor. Identify brooding tempests in the teacup of your situation. Do not allow small things to become big. If you sleep on your anger it will fester and grow. Be quick to make up and "make out." (An American way to say "love on each other"). When you are cranky it is time for "hanky-panky." A personal touch or a long, loving kiss can go far to change the mood.

Prayer Application

Dear Heavenly Father
Lord Help me to be the ultimate spouse for my Husband/Wife. Guide, protect and infuse us both with a greater love and understanding for one another. You have given us the ability to bring the best out in one another. May we love one another as selflessly as You love us. Help us to be a Magnificent Man and a Wonderful Woman, a true reflection of our God whom is both magnificent and altogether wonderful.
In Jesus name.
Amen.

Notes:

Chapter 16: Supernatural

Miracle Men And Wonder Women

Miracles do still happen. What is miraculous to man is second nature to God. Whenever He is involved we should expect His miraculous power to effect circumstances and impact lives. The Bible boldly declares,

"For with God nothing shall be impossible." [1]

The wonder of the Almighty is that He dwells[2] in us and empowers us[3] to do greater things[4] for Him. When Jesus was sending out His disciples He told them to,

> *"Preach, saying, the kingdom of heaven is at hand. Heal the sick, cleanse the lepers, and raise the dead, cast out devils: freely you have received, freely give."* [5]

Jesus was telling them to step into the realm of the impossible. They were to do the impossible together with God! Mountain Moving Men and Wave Walking Women are prepared to do just that. With activated faith, obedience to God and boldness that comes from the Holy Spirit we march on in spite of circumstances and obstacles. We move the mountains and walk on water. We expect the unexpected, predict the unpredictable and challenge the unchallenged. We are not content with the limitation problems might bring. We are not blinded by the facts in the realm of the natural. We peer into the realm where God abides, the realm of the Spirit and prepare and pray for signs, wonders and miracles.

We are not content with the limitation problems might bring. We are not blinded by the facts in the realm of the natural. We peer into the realm where God abides, the realm of the Spirit and prepare and pray for signs, wonders and miracles.

God is not a show-off. He does not need to convince anyone

---

1 Luke 1:37
2 John 15:4-7
3 Acts 1:8
4 John 14:2
5 Matthew 10:7-8

of His deity by performing miracles. That is not the purpose of miracles at all. Miracles happen because what God does is miraculous. His fingerprints are imprinted on such deeds, not because of the power of the deeds, but because of the mastery of His hands. Every miracle is attached to meeting a need. It is the solution to a problem, a healing to a sickness, an answer to a question, a way out for a captive soul. Miracles follow where God goes so if men and women follow Him with all their hearts they too will walk in the realm of the miraculous. Jesus said,

> *"And these signs will follow those who believe: In My name they will cast out demons; they will speak with new tongues; they will take up serpents; and if they drink anything deadly, it will by no means hurt them; they will lay hands on the sick, and they will recover. And they went out and preached everywhere, the Lord working with them and confirming the word through the accompanying signs."* [6]

Do you want the Lord to work with you, to join your efforts every day? Would you like to see His fingerprints in your life too? Then do what He wants you to do. Live a life of obedience and devotion to Him. Activate your faith in Him. When you need a miracle He will be there to perform it. He will confirm His word in your life with the signs following.

Do not just wait for the spectacular. Miracles are all around us. Creation is a miracle. Keeping planet earth on course around the sun is miraculous. Seeing seeds grow and children becoming who God made them to be is wondrous. Knowing God is a continual miracle. If He did not reveal Himself to you, you would not even know He existed. If He did not love you and Jesus did not die for your sins on the cross, you would not

---

6 Mark 16:17-18, 20 NKJV

have everlasting life! Why do birds fly, seasons change, rain fall and rivers flow? It is God's miracle of creation. What might be insignificant to you can be miraculous to someone else. And what might be miraculous in your life might be mundane to someone else.

Acquire the mentality of a mountain mover and a wave walker. Instill this attitude in your children. Decide not to buckle under the stress of life. Being a Mountain Moving Man and a Wave Walking Woman is a faith walk applied to everyday life. That is how we will become wonder working women and miracle making men. We do not work alone, but partner with God to see miracles happen.

If you want to experience more miracles in your life then identify needs and position yourself to see those needs met. Pray for the sick, believing for God's healing to flow. Expect to see miracles. Go make a difference in someone's life and credit God for all He has done. God in you enables you to move mountains. And God in you makes you buoyant to walk on waves. Remember life revolves around Him and not merely around what He does. This life is not simply about the miraculous but about the miracle of eternal life. What God has done for you, you can share with others. The abundant life He made available to you, He wants you to share with others. You can pass on the miracle of salvation. Go ahead and affect people's eternal outcome. Introduce them to Jesus. Share His amazing love with the world.

By being a Mountain Moving Man and a Wave Walking Woman you can change the landscape of faith in your neighborhood or job arena. Make a distinct difference in the world by sharing the miracle of Jesus to those around you. God's word is clear,

> *"For we are God's fellow workers."*[7]

---

7 1 Corinthians 3:9

Not only does He want to work with you, He invites you to work with Him! He has so many miracle projects going on all around you. Roll up your sleeves and let Him direct your doings and sayings. Do your part and He will certainly do His. Do not worry; you do not have to save them, Jesus will. You simply share your testimony as a first hand witness of the saving grace of God with them. Do not even try to heal them, simply share your faith with them and pray, believing Jesus will step in and accomplish what He alone can. He is your Senior Partner and you are His associate. Act on His behalf and in His authority, always pointing to Him because life revolves around Him.

Did you know that your word means much more to your long-time neighbor than the voice of a stranger? You have history with them, a reputation that gives leverage to God's cause in their lives. Use your influence for the glory of God. Help to position them to receive their own personal miracle from the Lord. Live in the realm of the remarkable and people will yearn for what you have to offer.

Join the multitude of Mountain Movers and Wave Walkers, husbands and wives the Lord is raising up in our generation, ordinary people with an extraordinary vision. Everyday people who choose to impact their world for God every day. Couples who have discovered the adventure of serving God together and are continually unlocking the blessings their unity brings. A perfect marriage is not a result of perfect people participating in it. It is the product of two imperfect people, living in an imperfect world, daring to believe in and serve a perfect God together.

Not only does He want to work with you, He invites you to work with Him! He has so many miracle projects going on all around you.

Make sure your faith is genuine and your testimony a true

reflection of who you are.

Preparing for a Miracle

There are so many things you can do to partner with God to see and experience more miracles in your life. Remember, God is calling you to be a Mountain Mover and a Wave Walker! Jesus spoke about both the mountains and the waves. He said,

> *"I tell you the truth, you can say to this mountain, 'May you be lifted up and thrown into the sea,' and it will happen. But you must really believe it will happen and have no doubt in your heart."* [8]

And,

> *"Yes, come," Jesus said. So Peter went over the side of the boat and walked on the water toward Jesus.* [9]

In both instances Jesus invited people to do the impossible! He expressed His desire to see them step into the realm of the miraculous. His words today also come to us as an invitation.

Witness God's power and be a witness of His deity.

To become a Mountain Moving Man and a Wave Walking Woman your first order of business is to accept His marvelous invitation.

Then you start to prepare your life for miracles. Instead of seeing the difficulty of your circumstances, focus on the greatness of God. Stop seeing a stumbling block, see a stepping stone. Expect miraculous change. When other focus on tough situations you see great opportunities for God to do wonders. Make room in your life for the manifestation of signs and wonders. You simply have to change the way you look at things.

---

8 Mark 11:23 NLT

9 Matthew 14:29 NLT

Look to God and not circumstances. See the need but focus your attention of Him. Stop looking at the size of the mountain before you or the magnitude of the wave you are facing. Sizing up mountains and waves against God will put things in the right perspective. He is so much bigger! In fact, there is no comparison between them. God is in a class of His own.

Now that your eyes are focused, tune your ears to the frequency of heaven. Ignore the negative criticisms and doubting voices. Stop listening to howling wind driving the waves. Listen to the voice of God and obey the Word of God. Apply what you hear to your situation and not vice versa. Remember the Word of God says,

> *"So then faith comes by hearing, and hearing by the Word of God."* [10]

When you listen to the Word of God your faith is activated to believe for the impossible to be manifested. God has a word of tremendous potential over your precarious situation.

Next, speak to the potential of God. Declare what you believe. Speak to the mountain and declare life in a death situation and healing amidst sickness. Faith declarations add actions to otherwise dead faith. Faith without works is dead[11] and the first action to faith should be the verbal declaration over your circumstances. Do not allow for doubting discussions and endless debates. Speak and address the situation.

Now, expect results! Stand back and make room for God to maneuver in. Do not get in His way. Remember miracles are still His specialty. You are not the miracle maker, He is. You are merely cooperating with Him. Apply your faith by waiting patiently and expectantly on Him.

---

10 Romans 10:17 NKJV

11 James 2:20

A very important aspect of walking in the realm of the miraculous is to constantly give glory to God. Thank Him for all He is doing in your life and testify of His glorious work and love. Witness His power and be a witness of His deity. Share His goodness and grace with others. That is probably the greatest way of bringing Him honor.

Join the multitude of Mountain Movers and Wave Walkers, husbands and wives the Lord is raising up in our generation, ordinary people with an extraordinary vision. Everyday people who choose to impact their world for God every day. Couples who have discovered the adventure of serving God together and are continually unlocking the blessings their unity brings. A perfect marriage is not a result of perfect people participating in it. It is the product of two imperfect people, living in an imperfect world, daring to believe in and serve a perfect God together.

You are called to be God's Mountain Mover and Wave Walker.

Prayer Application

Dear Heavenly Father
We desire to see Your miracles and wonders. Use our lives to showcase the greatness of our God. The miracle of Your love and grace has changed us. You are yesterday, today and forever the same. Allow us to walk on the waves just like Peter walked with You and displace the mountains / obstacles, like Moses parted the waters of the Red sea, in Your victorious power, make us Mountain Moving Men and Wave Walking Woman.
In Jesus name.
Amen.

Notes:

About the Authors

Rudi Swanepoel was born and raised in South Africa. He received a Divine calling for the full-time ministry in 1987 and started out in the ministry after extensive schooling at the Auckland Park Theological Seminary in Johannesburg. He earned a M.A. and D.Min from Christian Leadership University in Buffalo, NY.

He is a noted author and his books and unique practical teaching style is a favorite with international students. He is also an international lecturer, teaching in Seminaries and Colleges around the world. He is a sought after speaker at leadership development and staff training meetings.

He ministers the Word of God in a fresh and powerful way and is gifted to bring insight in the Word for young and old to understand. The Lord confirms his ministry with accompanying signs and wonders. He is ordained with the Assemblies of God in the USA. Rudi married Sharon in 1989.

Sharon Swanepoel is a native South African. She grew up in the Free State in South Africa She was very active in church from a young age and as a teenager she initiated a ministry of intercession which expanded quickly. They prayed every week and went out into the streets often to share the Gospel. Sharon studied at the Auckland Park Theological Seminary in Johannesburg, South Africa.

Sharon is a seasoned minister of the Gospel and has been a keynote speaker at various conferences and leadership training events both in the USA and abroad. She preaches the Word of God under a tremendous anointing and with great revelation knowledge. Her messages are practical and powerful.

She is an anointed musician / composer and ministers prophetically through her music. She is an accomplished trumpeter. She was a crusade singer at a Reinhard Bonnke Evangelistic Crusade in Kafanchan, Nigeria where the crowds grew to over 360,000 per service.

Through an extensive ministry of intercession she has seen many miracles that changed the lives of many people throughout the world. Today Sharon's music, like the Psalmists of old ushers you right into the Throne Room of God.

She is also the author of the children's book series: The Adventures of Seek and Save and founder of the Seek & Save Project, through which they print and distribute thousands of these Gospel books to the children of the world.

Sharon is ordained with the NXL Apostolic Network based in Youngstown, OH.

Together, Rudi & Sharon form a unique ministry team. Wherever they minister as one there is a shaking in the spiritual realm. Their passion is to see people connect to Jesus wherever they go. Their unity in marriage is evident in the way they live and enjoy life together.

Their desire is to see the Church healthy and effective in reaching the lost for Christ because they have a tremendous love for people.

In 1994 the Lord visited them supernaturally and instructed them to travel the world with His message of Glory and Power. Many people have been saved, delivered and healed through the ministry God gave them. This ministry will challenge people to rise up and be what God called them to be, walking in the power of the Holy Spirit continuously.

In every meeting throughout the world they see the lives of people being changed by God's Glory as they surrender to the will of the Lord.

Rudi & Sharon have inspired and motivated church leaders, pastors, professionals, and ministry leaders both on local and regional level. They have led many conferences, seminars, training / teaching events often with many churches participating together. Their ministry regularly crosses denominational, cultural and other boundaries to present the Gospel message of hope to the nations of the world.

For ministry information visit **GodsGlory.org**

Other Resources

Visit GodsGlory.org for ordering details

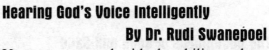

Books

Hearing God's Voice Intelligently

By Dr. Rudi Swanepoel

You were created with the ability to hear the voice of the Lord. In this book you will learn all about how God communicates. You'll discover and develop this amazing gift God gave you. It is informational and practical. It unlocks mysteries that was hidden for centuries. It will guide you to a lifestyle where hearing God's voice is the norm; to where every day is an adventure with God.

Mountains of God

By Dr. Rudi Swanepoel

The greatest events that shaped the course of history and humanity occurred on mountains. Abraham demonstrated His commitment to God on a mountain. Moses was called, instructed and impacted on a mountain. Elijah called fire from heaven on a mountain. Jesus taught and was transfigured on a mountain. He died on a hill and ascended to heaven from a mountain. He will return to earth and set His foot on a mountain. The Bible is teaming with stories of lives touched and changed as a result of mountain experiences.

This book recreates these momentous mountain moments and leads the reader to the apex of spiritual experience. In his unique riveting writing style, Rudi explores the importance of climbing these same mountains in a quest to partake of the glories God made available to those explorers of the greater things of the Kingdom of Heaven. Reading this book will introduce to you a whole new world of satisfying spiritual experiences based on Biblical truths. This book is an invitation and introduction to the Mountain of God.

The Adventures of Seek and Save
Lost At Sea

By Sharon Swanepoel

This is Sharon's first installment in a delightful new children's book series. It is about the adventures of two friends, Seek and Save, who partner together in rescuing people in need. This book is filled with adventure and comedy all set in rhyme.

The Adventures of Seek and Save
Lost In The Dark

By Sharon Swanepoel

Written in rhyme, this story is inspired and contains several valuable life lessons in obedience, conquering fear and the power of faith. Kids can test their memories on the "Quiz time with Tell" page and learn Scripture on the "Memory Verse" page. The book also has a prayer of salvation to help kids connect to Jesus. Get your copy today!

The Adventures of Seek and Save
The Village

By Sharon Swanepoel

Seek and Save is on Safari in the Kalahari. In this third installment of this powerful children's book series an entire African Village discover the power of Christ's forgiveness and salvation. This book is filled with life lessons and points kids to Jesus, the Author and Finisher of their faith. The prayer of salvation will connect them to Christ.

Music CD's

"See His Face" by Sharon Swanepoel

A CD that will thrust you into the presence of God. See His face is powerful and intimate, passionate and anointed and will lift your spirit, stir your heart and ignite your spiritual appetite for more of the Lord.

"I Wait" by Sharon Swanepoel

This CD is a collection of Psalms set to music. You'll memorize Scripture while basking in the wonderful anointing that accompanies these songs. Sharon has again succeeded to bring us a true soaking experience in the presence of God.

"Holy One" by Sharon Swanepoel

It is an intimate worship experience that will release a tremendous anointing into your life. Holy One is over an hour of warm worship, 9 original songs birthed in the presence of God. This CD is signature Sharon!

"Worship With Angels" By Sharon Swanepoel

This prophetic CD ushers you right into the Holy of Holies and invites you to worship with the angelic host. This recording came as a result of spontaneous moments in God's presence. It carries a tremendous anointing and will enhance you devotional time.

"Songs from the Heart" By Sharon Swanepoel

This CD has touched many lives. Recorded in South Africa it features the legendary song, Waterfalls of Praises, along with 9 other original songs by Sharon. Together these songs form Sharon's testimony of her early walk with God. Songs from the Heart is refreshing, professional and heart-warming. A perfect gift to a desponded heart!

Visit GodsGlory.org for ordering details